Nelson Mandela and the rise of the ANC

Compiled and edited by **Jurgen Schadeberg**

Photographs by
Ian Berry
Cloete Breytenbach
Bob Gosani
Ranjith Kally
Alf Kumalo
Peter Magubane
G R Naidoo
Gopal Naransamy
Jurgen Schadeberg

Text by
Benson Dyantyi
Albert Luthuli
Nelson Mandela
Bloke Modisane
Ezekiel Mphahlele
G R Naidoo
Philip Ngosana
Jordan Ngubane
Nathaniel Nkasa
Henry Nxumalo
Alan Rake
Can Themba

Jonathan Ball and Ad. Donker Publishers

Jonathan Ball Publishers
and
Ad. Donker Publisher
PO Box 2105
Parklands, 2121

© J R A Bailey 1990

All rights reserved. No part of this publication may be reproduced, stored in a retrieval system, or transmitted in any form or by any means, electronic, mechanical, photocopying, recording or otherwise, without prior permission from the publishers.

First published 1990

ISBN 0 947464 18 2

A Bailey's African Photo Archives Production
Executive editor: J R A Bailey
Editor/Designer: Jurgen Schadeberg
Photographic prints: Tracey Irwin
Layout: Adam Seftel
Archive researcher: Marié Human
Front cover: Colour photograph of Nelson Mandela by Paul Weinberg (Afrapix)
The three photographs facing Nelson Mandela are:
Top: Z K Matthews, *Middle:* Albert Luthuli, *Bottom:* Oliver Tambo
Reproduction, printing and binding: The Penrose Press, Johannesburg

Contents

Foreword   6
Walter M Sisulu

Foreword   7
Helen Joseph

Introduction   8
J R A Bailey

The evolution of a decade   10
Yusuf Cachalia

Preface   11
Jurgen Schadeberg

A closed and barred door: The search for peaceful change   13
Tim Couzens

From the pages of *Drum*   24

South Africa since Sharpeville 1960–1988   176
Njabulo S Ndebele

Nelson Mandela is released from prison   181
René du Preez

Some of the writers, photographers and editors from the pages of *Drum*   190

Foreword

One of the burning issues of the present day is the manner in which our history is presented. History is a continuous and systematic recording of important past events. It is part of the society, not just as we wish it to be, but rather a true reflection of life as it is.

In a country of complete inequality, where basic human rights are denied and where the majority of the population has no voice in the affairs of the nation, the distortion of peoples' history is inevitable, as has been the case in South Africa for centuries. It is only when we bear this in mind that we can begin to appreciate the invaluable service of this *Drum* compilation of pictorial articles.

1949 closed with a bang – the Programme of Action of 1949 was to transform the ANC into a mighty fighting machine. Gone were the days when the leadership of the ANC could rely on deputations and petitions. A new era had dawned. 1950 saw the beginning of a decade – the beginning of a challenge to the Nationalist Party and its apartheid policy.

1950 commenced with a series of strikes – locally and nationally. 1 May was declared 'Freedom Day' and a strike was called for the whole of the Transvaal in protest against the bans imposed on leaders such as Yusuf Dadoo and Sam Kahn. During the strike eighteen people were killed in different parts of the Reef by the police who were supposed to protect them. This precipitated a national strike.

An emergency conference was called by the ANC to which the following organisations were invited: the South African Indian Congress (SAIC), the African Peoples' Organisation (APO), the Communist Party of South Africa (CPSA) and the ANC Youth League. The conference took the decision to call a one-day strike to protest against police killings, the Suppression of Communism Act, which was before Parliament, and the Group Areas Act. The date was fixed for 26 June – the day the Suppression of Communism Act became law. This conference and its decision to go jointly into action was historic in many ways – in particular, it was to be the basis of future alliances and joint action.

The Defiance Campaign, which was launched on 26 June 1952, was carried out primarily by the ANC and the SAIC. In 1951 a joint National Planning Council had been appointed. It consisted of five members: Dr J S Moroka, J B Marks, and W M Sisulu for the ANC, and Dr Yusuf Dadoo and Yusuf Cachalia for the SAIC. These members, except for Dr Moroka, toured the main centres of the Union of South Africa collecting necessary material from local leadership for the purpose of recommendation to the respective conferences of the ANC and the SAIC. The plan of the Defiance Campaign and the commencement date of 26 June 1952 were accepted by the ANC conference in December 1951 and by the SAIC in January 1952.

Violence, which was used by the State in an attempt to crush the campaign, started in the Eastern Cape towards the end of 1952. In Port Elizabeth police attempted to arrest some young men for allegedly stealing paint. In East London the people had been granted permission by the authorities to hold a prayer meeting, but the police decided to break up the meeting and gave the people gathered only five minutes to disperse. Many people were killed in both instances. In Johannesburg and Kimberley, however, there were minor incidents of violence.

The Nationalist Party government used these events to introduce 'martial laws' such as the Public Safety and Criminal Law Amendment Act. In terms of these laws the government empowered itself to declare a State of Emergency and to impose heavy sentences on 'offenders'.

The Defiance Campaign was called off at the beginning of 1953 in the light of the new situation: more than 8 000 men and women had served various terms of imprisonment. Many of them were to form the core of dedicated and determined volunteers – a core that was to carry the struggle further in years to come. However, it was the Congress of the People that was not only to dominate but also to characterise not only the 1950s but the history of our struggle to the present day and to continue to be the programme of the future.

In recording and truthfully reflecting this history, *Drum* has therefore done remarkable work for posterity. In concluding, we must pay tribute to the African journalists of this period: they were truly worthy and fearless pioneers.

Walter M Sisulu

Foreword

It is more than thirty years ago that I stood on the steps of the Union Buildings in Pretoria watching twenty thousand women of all races, all colours, coming up the steps in a great mass. They came to make their protest to the Prime Minister, to tell him that they totally rejected passes for African women.

Now, three decades later, I am asked to write the foreword to a great book – and I appreciate the honour, and hope that I can do justice to the book. For these are great photographs that bring to life again those dauntless women, and the many others, men and women, who played their part in the 1950s, that wonderful decade of resistance to apartheid and oppression, the decade of solidarity and comradeship.

This great collection of photographs brings us the joy of meeting real people, the comrades who stood together, unforgettable moments of joy and sadness. And it is not only the inspired people who have, almost unbelievably, brought this book into being, sparing nothing of their strength, their labour and their time; it is also the unsung heroes who took the photographs, sometimes at physical risk, to whom we must pay tribute. For without them this book would not be, nor would any other pictorial record of our struggle exist.

It is difficult to find words which can adequately express the joy which these photographs bring, for they are more than just pictures. They bring real people out of the past for us to meet and greet. And I can say to myself, 'Yes, that's how we looked then, thirty years ago.' There are others who had gone from us, into exile, into gaol: Mandela, Tambo, Sisulu, but they have come back again. There are others who will never come again: Chief Luthuli, Z K Matthews, Lilian Ngoyi, Ruth First and so many others who have not lived to see the freedom for which we still struggle and which we know will come one day.

Looking through this book, I saw a face I knew, the face of a man who died not so long ago. It was James Phillips, the coloured president of the old Coloured Garment Workers Union of the Transvaal (see pages 31, 36, 44, 49, 53), and I remembered a story about him. During the 1950s, James was suddenly, cruelly struck down by a banning order under the Suppression of Communism Act. It forced him to resign from his union, and forbade him to enter any clothing factory again. For James this was the end. He was a skilled garment worker, he knew no other trade, and for him to give up his leadership, even his membership, of his union was a crippling blow. Somehow he had to be got out of South Africa, but he had no money, no passport. Friends worked hard; a French airline agreed to take him without documents. Standing with his mother, I watched him walk up the stairway and enter the plane. He was a free man again, and I knew that his glorious bass voice would once again sing freedom songs to the outside world.

The passenger steps were rolled away and the doors closed. The great aircraft began slowly to taxi out to the runway, and then it stopped. The stairway was brought back and the doors opened. We saw with horror as a car rushed out to the plane, and two men got out and raced up the stairs. I held James's mother tightly, the tears running down our faces. Was James going to be brought back to serve out the years of his ban? Then the men came out again, still only two of them, without James. The stairs were rolled away again and the plane took off. Later we heard that the Special Branch detectives had indeed come for James, but the Captain had told them curtly that they were now on French territory, and refused to hand him over.

The decade of the fifties was indeed not only the decade of non-violent resistance, but also the decade of the African National Congress. The ANC grew from strength to strength after the great Defiance Campaign and even during the first mass Treason Trial, from which the ANC emerged totally victorious.

You'll find it all in these photographs, and I am sure that even if you see these pictures for the first time ever, you cannot fail to be moved by the strength of our leaders, by the solidarity of the people, by the great love of our people and our country that bound us together, both then and for the future. Finally, I can only say, 'Thank you, *Drum* and its photographers, and you who have brought it all to life again'.

Helen Joseph

Introduction

Let us put the people and events described in this book on the ANC into some sort of historical perspective: my fellow introducers will discuss the more important people and events.

The rapidity with which everything has happened in Eastern and Southern Africa! As a boy I knew and photographed Colonel Frank Johnson, who took £90 000 off Rhodes and created Rhodesia. Today Harare is a gem of a city with more than three-quarters of a million inhabitants. My own father used to describe putting down duck-decoys and shooting partridges in the centre of what is now Johannesburg. Johannesburg today is a city of several million inhabitants: a city which could and should have been the industrial powerhouse for the whole of sub-Saharan Africa. Not so many years ago, we ran in *Drum East Africa* the story by an old Kikuyu of seeing the first white man appear in the so-called White Highlands of Kenya. Nairobi itself was founded in 1902. It is expected to be a city of four million people by the turn of the century.

Pictures taken by photographers at this period – by the trigger-happy Colonel Meinertzhagen, by the grandfather of John Fletcher in Rhodesia, by various photographers in South Africa – show Africans bollock-naked, armed with spears, knobkerries and shields. Now their grandchildren, given opportunity, make presidents, airline pilots, computer operators, bank managers: you name it, they do it. This rate of progress is unprecedented in any place at any time in history, and it has come from black and white working creatively together.

So if things go wrong – as they so often do – mistakes must be placed against their historical background. And, of course, anyone who takes over a large lump of Africa and calls it 'white man's country' is getting his knickers in a knot to begin with.

Cecil Rhodes gave an example to his fellow captains of industry that money was to be made for what general good it might produce. Diamonds and gold fuelled progress in Africa. So Beit built bridges and railways. My father gave scholarships, a wonderful art collection and helped to finance Winston Churchill – that key figure in world history – in his dark days. Before the end of the nineteenth century Rhodes had proclaimed: 'Equal rights for all civilised men'.

Although today's South African captains of industry, for the most part, wash hands with the government daily and have no greater ambition than making more and more money, it is nevertheless this economic development which is the real revolutionary factor in Africa. In the last thirty years, in Ghana and Guinea, Uganda and Tanzania, flags have changed, anthems have changed, newspapers have changed, slogans have changed. But as soon as you get off the high road into the villages and small towns, if anything has changed in thirty years, it is often for the worse. While in South Africa – a country which has been described as the only country in the world which could go forward by going backward – little has changed on the surface: flags, anthems, cops, newspapers, names in the newspapers. But at the grass-roots, due to the slowly rising standard of living, much has changed. The man who, as a child, rode behind a donkey and then bought himself a bicycle, sometimes owns a car. It is economic development which has brought this about and is the most meaningful revolutionary factor on the African continent. Gandhi wrote: 'To the poor, God comes in the form of bread.'

The mutual incomprehension of different cultures! It took me a long time to realise that the average black South African was a greater patriot, in the fullest sense of the word, than nearly all his white counterparts. And that almost every South African, black or white, was an imperialist at heart!

One morning, some time in the sixties, I ran into the head of the PAC in Nairobi – thus the head PAC 'terrorist' there. He invited me to have a coffee with him. Over coffee he began: 'Bailey, you know, the officers in the South African army have more brains than the officers in the other armies in Africa. What South Africa needs to do is to increase the army by about three times by bringing us black chaps into it, and we could take the whole continent.'

I at once reflected: Who are the real patriots in England? The toffs who become tax-exiles at the drop of a hat? Or the cockneys who believe that everyone and everything in Britain is superior to everywhere else? And is the situation any different in France between the *poilu* and the *rentier*? And are the real patriots in South Africa not the blacks?

All this goodness and goodwill has been thrown away by apartheid governments. At the time of writing this, the 150th anniversary of the Great Trek is being celebrated.

'All political parties in South Africa should endeavour to have emerged from the nineteenth century before the twenty-first arrives'

The celebrators have not noticed that under their government a second Great Trek on a greater scale has occurred. Their fellow-citizens are escaping the regime of systematic insult and humiliation that their government imposed. Under Smuts, South Africa was a country to which brains drained; under the Trekker government it quickly became a country from which brains drained. Yet the only worthy ambition must be to progress as swiftly in the future as has been progressed in the past: this requires a normal society with everyone contributing patriotically. A vision of future generations must become apparent, must become compulsive.

Social Engineering, Sociology, is a contradiction in terms. If it is about engineering, it has nothing to do with society: if it is about society, it has nothing to do with engineering. But the pretentious conjunction of these two words permitted intellectuals to use human beings like metals. Hendrik Verwoerd had been a Sociology lecturer at Stellenbosch University, so the moving of three million blacks, coloureds and Indians, and the bulldozing of their homes, was of the idiom. At precisely the same time, Julius Nyerere in Tanzania, Verwoerd's principal adversary, was forcibly moving six million Tanzanians for their own good: with the assistance and encouragement of sociologists from the left wing of the British Labour Party, who descended upon Dar es Salaam University and Kivikoni College to practise upon the unfortunate Tanzanians what they would never have been permitted to practise in Britain. At the time of writing this, Ceausescu is in the midst of the same horror in Romania. Forgotten are Immanuel Kant's words, central to European culture: 'Man shall be used as an end withal, never as a means only.' The humblest of electrical engineers has done more for the progress of society than the most illustrious of social engineers.

When one sits back and looks at the time-span this history of the ANC covers, one cannot fail to notice that for most of the time that the ANC was a non-violent organisation, there was a period of lunatic mass-killing across the world. The eighteenth century knew what the twentieth century forgot, that no human being is to be trusted with power. Lord Acton's oft-repeated words run: 'Power corrupts and absolute power corrupts absolutely.' So it is that the United States of America, because of its wise Constitution, runs pretty much the same whoever is President, while Hitler and Lenin set their countries on courses that ended in seas of blood. Despite this, we found a small number of devoted followers of Lenin, Comrade Mao and Joseph Stalin among the ANC, of Hitler devotees among Nationalist Ministers. In Hitler's war, fifty million died. Joseph Stalin, exploiting the political machinery that Lenin had created, murdered, according to the estimates of Solzhenitsyn, thirty million of his fellow Russians. Comrade Mao in China, the 'Great Helmsman', murdered, it is suggested in the Orient, between thirty and sixty million of his fellow Chinese during the so-called Cultural Revolution. Unprecedented butchery! In the last two cases perpetrated in the name of Social Engineering.

A normal society – and its political centre – is what the vast majority of *Drum*'s readers in South Africa who discussed these things with me, said they wanted. And could not get. 'We have only one life to lead, so far as we know. Let's be able to make as much of it as we can.'

Into our office in the fifties wandered a scattering of black politicians, gangsters, boxers, ladies of moderate virtue, Special Branch men concealed under one cloak or another, and so on. It was a period of comparative innocence, hopefulness. As Can Themba frequently quoted: 'It was the best of times, it was the worst of times.' The citizens of Johannesburg looked on themselves as being far more sophisticated than the Africans to the north. I heard the hopes expressed on a number of occasions that once the countries to the north had gained independence 'our folk' would be able to spearhead the commercial development of South Africa across the whole African continent. And *Drum* magazine was beautifully placed to carry this advertising, in both directions, from one side of Africa to the other. Instead, Dr Verwoerd said that the country north of the Limpopo was not 'white man's country' and he placed a tourniquet across the continent at the Limpopo River. As a result of this, both parts of the body have become gangrenous. The African Common Market still lies far ahead.

The former Israeli Foreign Minister, Abba Eban, who turned up in Accra when I was there, made a noteworthy observation: 'No government does the correct thing until it has exhausted all other alternatives'.

J R A Bailey

The evolution of a decade

If the 1940s in South African chronology represented a time when racial discrimination was enshrined in the statute books, the 1950s stand out as an era in which defiance of repugnant laws united thousands in heroic opposition to apartheid. It was as if the act of defiance had breathed new life into the bodies of the dispossessed. They had awakened with vigour and determination. They were champing at the bit – freedom was in sight, freedom in our lifetime! It was in this period that *Drum* made its mark, recording the agony and the anguish, the hopes and the fears, the joy and the jubilation of a people armed with an idea whose time had come.

It was as if the very act of oppression had sown the seed of resistance and it was the task of the newly-formed Congress Alliance – the ANC and South African Indian Congress (SAIC) – to revive the resistance, to harness it and channel it through a decade of defiance. On 26 June 1952 these two organisations launched the Defiance Campaign. The progress of the Campaign was monitored and directed by the National Action Council. Daily meetings were held by Walter Sisulu, Nelson Mandela, Oliver Tambo, Moses Kotane, Yusuf Dadoo, Molvi Cachalia and myself. We liaised with the provincial and regional congresses and coordinated the national Campaign. During the course of the Campaign, the Congress of Democrats (COD) and the Coloured Peoples' Organisation (CPO) were formed.

The response of the government was to arrest twenty leaders of the Campaign. They were tried, found guilty and received suspended sentences. The Campaign continued in spite of the government's attempts to thwart it. The State had alleged, but failed to prove, that the Defiance Campaign was communist inspired. Proof of the Campaign's broad base was provided by Father Huddleston, later Archbishop of the Indian Ocean and President of the British Anti-Apartheid Movement. Huddleston initiated weekly meetings with Bishop Ambrose Reeves, Rabbi Rabinowitz, Molvi Cachalia, Oliver Tambo and myself. The purpose was to monitor and ensure that the Campaign proceeded peacefully. The protest, despite its peaceful nature, seemed to spur the government to embark on further acts of aggression and dispossession. Strijdom had succeeded Malan in December 1954 and the Nationalist Party embarked on a policy of relentless pursuance of naked white *baasskap*.

Regardless of the acceleration of apartheid, Congress was on the march. After the Defiance Campaign, the joint executives of the ANC, the SAIC, the CPO and the COD met in Natal. It was here that the idea of a Congress of the People was presented by the ANC. A joint consultative committee comprising the four congresses was set up. This committee consisted of Walter Sisulu, Duma Nokwe, Stanley Lollan, Ruth First, Rusty Bernstein, A Patel and myself. We were entrusted with the task of organising the Congress of the People.

Those were heady days: in February 1955 Sophiatown was demolished, and in March the South African Congress of Trade Unions (SACTU) was formed. In June the Congress of the People took place in Kliptown. It was here that the Freedom Charter was adopted by some 3 000 delegates from all areas of South Africa. The joint consultative committee had extended invitations to the Nationalist Party and the United Party. They declined to attend. The Congress movement set about publishing the Freedom Charter as the firm basis of the movement for national liberation. In March 1956 a special ANC conference adopted the Freedom Charter and in August 20 000 women marched on Pretoria to petition Strijdom. In December the government arrested 156 leaders for treason. The trial went on for over four years resulting in the acquittal of all the accused. Oswald Pirow, wartime Nazi supporter and chief prosecutor in the Treason Trial, believed that the trial had resulted in a decline in agitation. He went on to remark that if there would be any serious threat to white rule the 'shooting of 5 000 natives would provide quiet for a long time to come'. Nevertheless, Pirow and the Nationalists were unable to foresee or stem the protest of 50 000 Africans in Alexandra township who began a bus boycott in January 1957.

Later that year Hendrik Verwoerd said, 'We will use an iron hand against those who undermine the government's apartheid policy.' He was true to his word. His government set about the implementation of Grand Apartheid, and banned the ANC in April 1960. The history of the period shows that the government's draconian attempts to block the winds of change blowing across the African continent made peaceful opposition almost impossible. One year after Sharpeville, Mandela and others abandoned the ANC's policy of non-violence, and in December 1961 'Umkhonto we Sizwe' began its campaign of sabotage and distributed its manifesto. So ended the decade: a history of the evolution of South African politics from protest to challenge.

Yusuf Cachalia

Preface

The main body of this book, from pages 24 to 175, is filled with photographs and text taken straight from the *Drum* archives. In those cases where the photographs actually used in *Drum* were missing, I have substituted photographs of the same event or person, remaining as truthful as possible to the portrayal of events by *Drum*.

Apart from cutting the text for space reasons, and correcting the odd fact, almost all the articles by the *Drum* writers I have kept unchanged. In a few exceptional cases, for continuity reasons, I have had to condense two or more articles into one.

This book is a reflection of the ANC movement and the political and social conflict that existed during the fifties and early sixties in South Africa, seen through the eyes and minds of the *Drum* photographers and writers. The book does not attempt to give a total and exact history of the ANC or the political events of the period, but rather a greater insight into the courage, the hopes and fears, the disappointments, the energy and vitality that were erupting during a decade that might be remembered as one of the most dynamic periods in recent South African history.

During this period of extreme racism, and of a self-conscious, persistent awareness of people's racial background in South Africa, everyone was classified, named and stamped according to his or her colour.

Whites were called Europeans, although they might have been in South Africa, like many of the Afrikaners, for ten generations or more. The so-called Europeans were the Afrikaners (a mixture of early Dutch, French and German settlers), the English, Scots, Welsh and Irish, the Germans, the Portuguese from Madeira (who ran the greengrocery empires), the Greeks (who were in total control of all tearoom shops) and any others with Caucasian looks.

Non-Europeans were broken up into Asians or Indians (who were originally brought from India to Natal by British sugar farmers), the coloureds from the Cape, Hottentots, Bushmen, Malays and blacks.

The majority of the population consisted of a large number of African tribes, the main ones being Zulu, Xhosa and Sotho. Officially they were referred to as Bantu, meaning 'people' in Zulu. Farmers referred to them as *Kaffirs* and most whites called them Natives, addressing individuals as 'boy' or 'girl'. Blacks at the time preferred to call themselves Africans.

Today blacks are blacks and whites are whites. Maybe one day in the future we will have Anglokaners, Zulukaners, Boerekaners and Indiakaners.

During the early fifties in South Africa there were virtually no photographers reporting or recording events in the non-white world. Consequently people accepted and welcomed, without suspicion, the lonely photographer. Even the authorities, courts and police let me get on with it. They were puzzled why this crazy man bothered to photograph blacks. Only later in the mid-fifties did it become more difficult to record political events. When police were present, the photographers, especially black photographers, were often beaten up and arrested.

One of my first assignments on *Drum* was to take a cover picture of the glamorous film star and blues singer Dolly Rathebe. We decided to climb up a mine dump on the edge of a Johannesburg middle-class suburb. The dump consisted of a fine whitish sand and Dolly, in her bikini, posed for the cover in front of a beach-like background. Suddenly, from several directions, a number of police charged us, ordering us to stand still while the excited policemen inspected the sandy ground for marks and prints. We were taken to the police station under suspicion of contravening the Immorality Act. It was against the law for non-white and white to have sexual relations, and the punishment was nine months' imprisonment. After several hours and phone calls, we were finally released.

I wish to give my thanks to the people who helped and assisted me in producing this book, especially Adam Seftel for layout, Susan Steyn for her help with the text, Tim Couzens for his valuable advice and Jim Bailey for his guidance. Also Stan Motjuwadi, Yusuf Cachalia, Helen Joseph and Roy Christie.

Jurgen Schadeberg

The early leaders of the ANC were trained at overseas and local schools

R W Msimang (4th in row three) – one of the lawyers who founded the ANC – at school in Taunton, England.

Z K Matthews (standing left) at Lovedale School in the Eastern Cape.

Prologue: The ANC story 1912 – 1952

A closed and barred door: The search for peaceful change

In November 1952, Albert Luthuli was faced with an ultimatum by the South African government. Either he must resign from the African National Congress (ANC) or he would lose his chieftainship. It was a sad choice reflecting the erosion over the previous half-century of traditional chiefly power. He had little hesitation in accepting dismissal and, of course, his people continued to support him anyway. Within a month he was elected President-General of the ANC. But the decision concerning his chieftainship was symbolic of the change that had come about in regard to the nature of black society since the turn of the century. Over that period the intensity of discriminatory laws against Africans, coloureds, Indians and even some whites had intensified to the extent that Luthuli believed the stage had been reached where blacks had 'almost no rights at all'. The history of the period up to 1950 is one of a desperate search for any and every avenue of peaceful opposition to these laws as well as resistance or accommodation to the vast dynamics of the more hidden flow of social processes. Luthuli had come to the point, he said in criticising the government decision, where 'I have joined my people in the new spirit that moves them today, the spirit that revolts openly and boldly against injustice and expresses itself in a determined and non-violent manner.' That new revolt was the Defiance Campaign. In looking back over the decades that preceded it, Luthuli could only believe in its justness. 'In so far as gaining citizenship rights and opportunities for the unfettered development of the African people, who will deny that thirty years of my life have been spent knocking in vain, patiently, moderately and modestly at a closed and barred door?'

Who, indeed, can deny that the provocation was great? Luthuli, after all, was little different from the men who met on those bright summer days in Bloemfontein in January 1912, to found the South African Native National Congress (later the African National Congress). They were mostly mission-educated Christians and amongst them was a representative sample of chiefs. They all regarded themselves as 'progressive', eager to adapt to a new world, with an optimistic belief in a gradual evolution to full equality and political rights for all 'civilised' men. The initiative for the meeting had come from a young lawyer called Pixley Seme. While accepting the missionary's version of history that Africa had dwelt in a 'sleep of ages', Seme had his own dream:

O Africa!
Like some great century plant that shall bloom
In ages hence, we watch thee; in our dream
See in the swamps the Prospero of our stream;
Thy doors unlocked, where knowledge in her tomb
Hath lain innumerable years in gloom.
Then shalt thou, walking with that morning gleam,
Shine as thy sister lands with equal beam.

Some discriminatory legislation was already in place, such as that to do with passes, vagrancy, poll-taxes and liquor. The most crucial of all – exclusion from the franchise for most blacks – came with the establishment of the Union of South Africa in 1910.

The first major test for the new organisation soon presented itself. Building on earlier ideas of segregation – in particular those of the South African Native Affairs Commission of 1903 to 1905 – the Union government embarked on a policy of territorial segregation, laying aside land for the exclusive use of whites and blacks (the latter being restricted to less than ten per cent of the country). Thousands of families of tenant farmers were forced off white-owned land, either into the 'scheduled areas' or into the towns. In the famous words of Solomon Plaatje, one of the founders of the ANC: 'Awaking on Friday morning, 20 June 1913, the South African native found himself, not actually a slave, but a pariah in the land of his birth.'

Channels for opposing the 1913 Natives' Land Act and other discriminatory measures were limited. Even had the leaders of the ANC been of radically different ideological temperament, open resistance since the crushing of the Bambatha uprising in 1906 was no longer an option. The impact of the black vote in the Cape was proved negligible, and access to the law courts was manipulated and ineffective. The independence of some separatist churches was marginalised. Only the women, under the leadership of Charlotte Maxeke, achieved some success in their campaign of refusal to carry passes. Lobbying, however weak, was the only alternative. Delegations visited Britain in 1909 (to protest against political exclusion from the Act

Prominent founders of the ANC were also pioneering journalists

Solomon Plaatje, first Organising Secretary of the ANC. He founded the newspaper Koranta ea Becoana *in Mafeking in 1901.*

John Dube, first President of the ANC. He started an independent school, Ohlanga, in Natal in 1901, and the newspaper Ilanga Lase Natal *in 1903.*

After the 1913 Land Act, the ANC began to look to the outside world for allies

The South African Native National Congress delegation to England, June 1914. Left to right: Thomas Mapikela, Rev Walter Rubusana, Rev John Dube, Saul Msane, Sol Plaatje. The delegation tried to get the British government to intervene against the Land Act but the outbreak of the First World War thwarted their hopes.

of Union), 1914 (to persuade the British government to act against the Natives' Land Act), and 1919 (to seek allies for black interests in the aftermath of the First World War). Although these delegations were unsuccessful in their primary purposes, they were early attempts to turn world opinion in favour of the rights of the downtrodden.

Locally, protest found expression in the columns of black newspapers, particularly those owned by early ANC founders, John Dube and Solomon Plaatje. But their circulation was relatively small and, to a large extent, regional. Consequently, the ANC began its own newspaper, *Abantu-Batho*, in 1913. Published in Johannesburg, this newspaper's radicalisation of its editorial policy during the war years seems to have reflected changes in the nature of the African work force and a shift towards urban concerns. New tactics of resistance began to emerge.

The period 1917 to 1922 was one of great upheaval in South Africa. In 1918 workers engaged in the Shilling Strike, demanding an increase in wages. In 1919 the ANC, following the precedent of their women and of the Gandhi-inspired Indians, organised a passive resistance campaign in defiance of the pass laws. Several demonstrators were shot by the police, and no change in the laws resulted. In 1920 the ANC had a hand in the organisation of the first of South Africa's three great African mineworkers' strikes. But in many ways the original leadership of the ANC began to be left behind by circumstances.

Mindful of the recent revolution in Russia, and worried by the influence of the radical populist ideas being articulated in America by Marcus Garvey, a number of whites took fright and, believing revolution to be imminent, concluded that the edge must be taken off the thrust of the more radical leadership. They were helped in this by the visit of the American-educated West African, James Aggrey, who preached moderation and recommended the introduction of interracial debating societies, called Joint Councils. A number of other institutions were designed to foster the growth of a tamer black middle class. The Chamber of Mines, just as nervous, started a newspaper, *Umteteli wa Bantu*, in opposition to *Abantu-Batho*, and since it was distributed free it substantially undercut the ANC newspaper.

The 1920s witnessed stronger efforts by the Pact and Nationalist governments to impose the colour bar in industry and to extend land segregation. In 1923 influx control was tightened through the Urban Areas Act, and blacks were further restricted from freehold rights in urban areas. In 1926 Prime Minister Hertzog introduced four Native Bills threatening to deprive blacks of their direct vote. Some of the ANC turned to white liberals for allies, others to the communists. In 1927 James Gumede, the ANC President, visited Europe and the Soviet Union. But the most successful movement of the decade was the Industrial and Commercial Workers Union, the ICU, under Clements Kadalie and A W G Champion, which swept through town and countryside alike. Its growth was rapid, its demise (through organisational failures) equally so. Any chance of Gumede changing the direction of the ANC was stopped when he was replaced by the more conservative Seme in 1930.

Independent newspapers had also fallen on evil days. The first black-owned, black-run paper, *Imvo Zabantsundu*, had been started in the Eastern Cape in 1884. John Dube had begun *Ilanga Lase Natal* in 1903. Both were still going, but only just. *Abantu-Batho* was about to expire. All were in financial difficulty and the Great Depression was, like a doleful bailiff, just around the corner.

As President, Seme was little short of a disaster. Far from stimulating the regenerative awakening he had predicted twenty years before, he and his organisation aestivated in the dog days of a long complacency. Any of the doctors who were members of the ANC at the time, like Moroka or Molema, could have pronounced the ANC clinically dead.

In 1931 a young white, B G Paver, seized the opportunity to buy *Imvo* and *Ilanga* and started a company called Bantu Press to run them. He also started the first national newspaper for blacks, *Bantu World*. Its editorial policy was distinctly and consciously 'moderate' and, although its circulation increased fairly strongly, it meant that blacks had lost control of their own press.

Consequently, when in 1935 the ringmaster Hertzog decided his parliamentary support was strong enough to crack his whip and restart the whole circus of Native Bills, the old guard could not bestir themselves either to perform or resist. The threat was real. In return for an increase to

The period 1917–1920 was one of great unrest

In 1919 ANC leaders were arrested in Johannesburg during a strike.

In 1920 the ANC was involved in the huge mineworkers' strike

In the 1920s numerous efforts were made to moderate the radicalism of some of the leaders. The Bantu Men's Social Centre was founded in Johannesburg in 1924.

The ANC in 1928

Every year from 1912 to 1960 the ANC met in Bloemfontein, the geographic centre of South Africa.

Pixley Seme as a young lawyer. He was one of the founders of the South African Native National Congress, which later became the ANC.

Davidson Don Tengo Jabavu, who was President of the All African Convention in 1936.

During the war, the offices of **Bantu World** *were bombed by the Ossewabrandwag. When the war ended and victory was celebrated, many blacks began to realise that the struggle was only just beginning.*

Poet Herbert Dhlomo wrote:

Not for me the Victory celebrations!
Not for me,
Ah! Not for me,
I who helped and slaved in the protection
of their boasted great civilisation;
Now I sit in tears 'mid celebrations
Of a war I won to lose,
Of a peace I may not choose.

13 per cent of land for the exclusive use of blacks, Hertzog – in line with his policy of political as well as territorial segregation – proposed to remove the black voters from the common voters' roll and allow them to vote only for a limited number of white representatives.

In December 1935, frustrated by the weakness of the ANC, a new grouping met in Bloemfontein. Many, but by no means all, of its members belonged to the Congress. It named itself the All African Convention, and elected Professor D D T Jabavu as its president. The Convention rejected trusteeship, suggesting that the denial to the African people of participation in the government of the country on the basis of common citizenship was not only immoral and unjust but would also 'inflame passions and fertilise the soil on which the propagandists sow the seeds of discontent and unrest' and 'respectfully requested' the government to consider the advisability of such steps. But it stopped short of advocating universal franchise, substituting instead the willingness to accept the 'imposition of an education or property or wage qualification, as a condition for the acquirement of political privileges'.

The year had not been a good one for Africans. At various times some efforts had been made for closer contact with the rest of Africa. Pan Africanist ideas surfaced now and then. Abyssinia had been the one African country to avoid colonialism and to retain its independence. But, in October, the Italians invaded. Black South Africans waited eagerly to see whether Mussolini would be repulsed. For a brief moment *The African Liberator*, a new newspaper, sold thousands of copies. Its editor Gilbert Coka, was, at least publicly, confident: 'The hour of African freedom has struck. That for which Toussaint L' Ouverture suffered and died, that for which Frederick Douglass and Booker Washington lived and died, that for which Menelik, Shaka, Makana, Lewanika, Lobengula, Langalibalele and other great sons of Africa lived, suffered and died. The complete liberty of Africans to shape their own destiny in their own way has come. The light of liberty has broken in great splendour.' But the Abyssinians failed to roll back the Italian tide; the AAC failed to prevent the Hertzog bills becoming law.

The long winter of another World War brought its icy grip of hardship and discontent. 'Even firewood has gone to war', was a frequent complaint of the poor. People began to express their discontent in bus boycotts and squatters' movements, as the inexorable march to the cities continued.

In 1940 the ANC elected Dr A B Xuma as its president, a move which signalled a gradual revival in its fortunes. Xuma was no radical but he was an astute and cautious organiser and he lifted the ANC out of a state of bankruptcy. In 1943 with the publication of its document 'Africans' Claims in South Africa' – based partly on the Atlantic Charter – the organisation began to clarify its aims and direction for the first time in many years. Lamenting that Africans had 'no freedom of movement, no freedom of choice of employment, no right of choice of residence and no right of freedom to purchase land or fixed property from anyone and anywhere', the document affirmed faith in, indeed the right to, the 'four freedoms' and for the first time, categorically demanded 'the extension to all adults, regardless of race, of the right to vote and be elected to Parliament'. Democracy was, after all, the stated war aim of the Allies, and it was what many thousands of black soldiers were supposedly fighting for. The pariah was determined to come in from the cold. However, no strategy for achieving the aims of these claims was delineated by the ANC.

From as early as the passing of the Hertzog Acts in 1936, there were the first stirrings of political events within the ANC which would eventually replace the stand of the old guard. Many of the younger adherents began to be restless, waiting for a new spring. Finally, in 1944, they formed themselves into the Youth League within the Congress. And so the names of Mandela, Sisulu, Tambo, Mda and others began to find their way firstly onto the crucial committees and then into the people's consciousness. The Youth League was strongly supported by Jordan Ngubane's Durban-based newspaper *Inkundla ya Bantu*.

Debate in the 1940s centred around the relative merits of the strategies of Africanist exclusivity or multi-racial alliances. Initially, the Youth League, under the presidency of the charismatic Anton Lembede, urged the need for African assertion of African concerns and claims. This ambiguity between Africanism and multi-racialism can be seen, for instance, in the work of the most representative

New heroes began to emerge. There were the big swing bands of the 1930s and 40s. The Jazz Maniacs were amongst the most popular. They played for the armed forces during the war and became known as the Jazz Forces. Their leader (seen here on the left playing the saxophone) was Wilson Silgee who became famous as King Force.

Libraries were not open to blacks, so the Carnegie Library for blacks was started in Germiston. Here, inspecting a travelling outlet, is the first librarian, H I E Dhlomo, poet, journalist and the 'father' of black drama. In 1921, black literacy was about 9 per cent; in 1931 it was over 12 per cent; after the Second World War it had probably doubled. This expansion of the reading public provided the opportunity for new magazines like Zonk and Drum.

Josiah Gumede, President of the ANC. He was replaced by Seme.

Dr Alfred Bilini Xuma, politician and physician. After his freelance political activities in the thirties, Dr Xuma was elected President of the ANC in 1940. He set about rebuilding a scattered organisation against great opposition. Dr Xuma was a Drum director during the fifties.

Dr James Moroka, who replaced Dr Xuma as President of the ANC in 1949.

Albert Luthuli at the age of 25. Luthuli was President of the ANC from 1952 to March 1960, when the ANC was banned. Chief Luthuli won the Nobel Peace Prize in 1961.

poet and dramatist of the time, H I E Dhlomo. It was a perennial concern which had emerged in the 1920s and which was to lead to the eventual founding of the PAC in 1959 and give impetus to the Black Consciousness Movement of the 1970s.

But the dominant strand in the ANC retained its commitment to multi-racialism, a position from which it has never subsequently wavered. The ANC had already allied itself with various coloured groups in the Western Cape to form the Non-European Unity Movement. Now the terrible 1949 clashes between Africans and Indians in Durban drew the ANC and the Indian Congress together. The second great African mineworkers' strike in 1946 and the advent of the Nationalist government in 1948 had also pushed the ANC towards greater militancy. The independence of India also provided hope and the possibility of an end to colonialism.

Dr Xuma's visit to the United Nations in 1946 was the first step in that body's continuous search for sympathy for the position of the ANC. The coming to power of the Nationalist Party elbowed aside any hopes that government would follow Hofmeyr's more liberal tendencies, and the stage was set for more direct confrontation.

At last, at its meeting in 1949, the Congress formulated a decisive programme of action. This document urged the appointment of a council of action which would employ the weapons of 'immediate and active boycott, strike, civil disobedience, non-cooperation and such other means as may bring about the accomplishment and realisation' of Congress's aspirations. At the same meeting, with the help of the Congress's Youth League, Dr Moroka replaced Dr Xuma as president. Moroka was not the Youth League's ideal candidate but his succession did represent a crucial shift of power to the Youth League.

The Old Guard had reached the end of the road. They had to be replaced. Yet the younger generation owed them a great debt. The Old Guard had, after all, founded the ANC back in 1912. They had managed to start it with a large measure of unity and legitimacy. They had managed to keep it going even when its demise seemed inevitable. They had begun the long process of appealing to world opinion. (Ironically, the establishment of a permanent ANC presence overseas and the long road to sanctions only came about with the banning of the ANC in 1960.) They had managed to create a mansion with rooms wide enough to accommodate clergymen and communists, young and old, black, white, coloured and Asian.

Laws such as the Riotous Assemblies Act began to take effect. African communists, J B Marks and Moses Kotane, had certain banning restrictions placed on them in 1950. A May Day stay-away to protest against this action ended in the deaths of nineteen people. This stole some of the thunder in the Transvaal from the national work stoppage day called 'South African Freedom Day' scheduled for 26 June. But in Port Elizabeth and Durban the response was impressive.

The pursuit of apartheid ground its way remorselessly onward: the Group Areas Act, the Population Registration Act, the Suppression of Communism Act, the banning of mixed marriages, the enforced segregation of all facilities. The assault on people's lives, public and private, was formidable. In reply, the ANC and other groups formulated the greatest passive resistance campaign in the history of South Africa. Volunteers were deliberately to defy certain laws, above all, the pass laws. The campaign began symbolically on 6 April 1952, the 300th anniversary of the landing of Jan van Riebeeck at the Cape. Boycotts and rallies were held and, in the subsequent months, the process of law defiance gathered momentum. The events ensured that the ANC acquired a mass following and won its way into the hearts of the majority of South Africans. It remained to be seen whether its passive resistance tactics and peaceful means were strong enough to bend the hearts or break the backs of the ruling authorities.

The same growth of mass movements in the political and social arena led to changes in the outlook and composition of the press geared to a black audience. Under the editorship of an extreme Africanist and conservative elderly editor, R V Selope Thema, the *Bantu World* was lukewarm towards the ANC. In addition, its rather drab pages and lay-out matched its distinctly verbal approach. Over the decades the expansion of literacy had led to the creation of a small but significant post-World War middle class and a larger and more articulate working class. The ANC never managed to start a replacement for the late *Abantu-Batho*. But it was well served in the fifties by a new, enormously popular, independent magazine. *Drum* not only changed gear in the style and tempo of writing for its African audience, but it introduced the immediacy of investigative reporting. Most important of all, it gave primacy to the photograph. For the first time both the leadership and the rank and file of the ANC were not merely disembodied voices, words on a page, but real people. For a number of years, before the vicious and literally dehumanising effects of censorship took its toll, *Drum* and *Post* gave the people of the ANC and other organisations a human face.

Professor Tim Couzens

Left to right: The Old Guard in this historic picture are Dr Xuma, unknown, unknown, R V Selope Thema, Professor Z K Matthews, Paul Mosaka, Nobel Prize winner Albert Luthuli, and Dr J S Moroka.

December 1951

The ANC holds its annual conference at Bloemfontein

Drum: February 1952 In mid-December last year in Batho location, Bloemfontein, the African National Congress (ANC) held what may prove to be its most important session since its foundation nearly forty years ago. It was the first meeting since the abolition of the Natives' Representative Council (NRC), from which Congress leaders had resigned. The conference was characterised by many outspoken statements and important decisions and could well be looked back on as a turning point in the history of the Congress. Delegates endorsed the report of the Joint Planning Council, established in June last year, on a strategy of resistance to the six 'unjust laws'.

The Defiance Campaign was born in mid-1951, when non-white leaders met and formed a Joint Planning Council to plan a strategy for co-ordinating Africans, Indians and coloureds in an immediate mass campaign for the repeal of oppressive measures. The 'oppressive measures' they chose to protest against were limited to the pass laws, stock limitation, the Group Areas Act, the Separate Voters' Representation Act, the Bantu Authorities Act and the Suppression of Communism Act.

The Joint Planning Council consisted of Dr Moroka, J B Marks and Walter Sisulu of the ANC, and Dr Yusuf Dadoo and Yusuf Cachalia of the South African Indian Congress (SAIC). They issued a report, to be put before the ANC, proposing that the government be called on to repeal the unjust laws. If it refused, mass demonstrations were to be held followed by defiance of the laws.

On 17 December at its Bloemfontein conference, the ANC approved the report, and the campaign had begun. Dr Moroka demanded that the Prime Minister, Dr Daniel Malan, repeal the laws.

The Congress is now regarded as the national political movement of the African people throughout the Union, and the abolition of the NRC has awakened the masses of Africans to the realisation that their freedom will come from their own national movements.

One of the most important issues for the future is the question of unity among non-Europeans as a whole. The Congress, being essentially African and Nationalist, has not been quite ready to combine with other non-Europeans. But important changes are already coming about. The Congress is coming to see more clearly the necessity for working closely with other non-Europeans. The proposals for joint planning, particularly with Indians, have met with some opposition, notably from the Natal delegates, and less important but more publicised, from the 'Nationalist Bloc' of Transvaal. The *Bantu World*, edited by Richard Selope Thema, leader of the bloc, described such co-operation as an 'unholy alliance', and compared supporters of the alliance to 'a drowning man holding on to a shark'. But many people feel that it is more like two drowning men rescuing each other by keeping together.

Close co-operation between non-Europeans must be of the first importance, and the appearance of Yusuf Cachalia, Secretary of the South African Indian Congress, and Manilal Gandhi, Editor of *Indian Opinion*, on the dais at the Congress, was an interesting indication. The financial plight of the Congress would seem to show how ill she can afford to be insular and stand-offish from other non-Europeans. □

Henry Nxumalo

In his presidential address to Congress, Dr Moroka showed himself clearly on the side of the moderates, and stressed the need for continued attempts at co-operation with Europeans. At the same time he was firm in advocating compulsory education, freedom of movement, freedom to do any kind of work, and a say in legislation. And insistence on these four points forms the basis of the Congress's official policy.

*'The pass laws must go,' says Dr Moroka in his presidential address to Congress,
'if South Africa is to make any progress along the path of racial harmony and peace.
They are an iron chain forged for the enslavement of the African'*

Photographs by Jurgen Schadeberg

The proposals for the Defiance Campaign are approved

Moroka: Moderate but firm

'From the government of South Africa we ask for nothing that is revolutionary. If what we ask for is communistic, then communism is humane and Christian; it is a consummation devoutly to be wished. We ask for those things which, I believe, will facilitate co-operation between the Europeans and the non-Europeans.' On Dr Moroka's left is Rev Nimrod Tantsi, the political predikant.

'We ask for education for the Africans . . . education of the kindergarten type, primary education, secondary education, university education, technical and adult education . . . educational facilities commensurate with the African population of this land . . .'

Photographs by Jurgen Schadeberg

About 350 ANC delegates attended the conference. Congress Youth League National Secretary, Joe Matthews, said that more than half of them were closely connected with the trade unions. D W Bopape is addressing the conference from the floor.

Professor Z K Matthews, Cape President of the ANC since 1949. 'Addressing political meetings in the Cape, I have noticed that the political temper of the people is very high. In the Transvaal people are even more politically minded, but also tend to be more divided. They have many more groups of different tribal backgrounds.'

Dr S M Molema, ANC Treasurer. Dr Molema stressed that as the Congress is an organisation of the African working class with only a negligible number of professionals, there was need for a closer alliance between the Congress and African trade unions.

Walter Sisulu, ANC Secretary-General: 'Congress is in fact nationalist and concerned with the national oppression at home. For this reason the Congress naturally identifies itself with the people of the East who are in sympathy with our cause.'

J B Marks, ANC President, Transvaal. 'The struggle which the national organisations of the non-European people are conducting is not directed against any race or national group. It is against the unjust laws which keep in perpetual subjection and misery vast sections of the population. It is for the creation of conditions which will restore human dignity, equality and freedom to every South African.'

Photographs by Jurgen Schadeberg

ANC Youth League President, Nelson Mandela (with Ruth First, right): 'The white people of South Africa are steeped in the Herrenvolk philosophy of the "master race". In a multiracial society such as we find in South Africa, this sort of philosophical outlook breeds certain undesirable and even dangerous pathological attitudes and reactions. It breeds the myth of racial supremacy. It breeds the complex of individual superiority.'

Dr Moroka gives his views in an exclusive *Drum* interview

Q: *Dr Moroka, your speech gave the impression to many people, including the press, of being very moderate in tone. Was this intentional?*

A: Yes, I pleaded wisely. I myself believe that the Europeans in this country have come to stay, and that co-operation with Europeans is essential. It is impossible to have a lot of small and separate civilisations existing in the same country.

Q: *Do you consider that Congress is making good progress?*

A: At present the government is beating us. The Chiefs still retain their influence over most of the African people and the Chiefs do what the government tells them.

Q: *What is the ANC's attitude at present towards other non-Europeans?*

A: We in Congress believe we must organise our own people first, and co-operate with other non-Europeans from there. We want to retain our identity. We wish to co-operate fully but not combine.

Q: *With regard to the programme of mass action planned for early this year, will the methods you envisage be similar to those employed recently by Mr Gandhi?*

A: Yes, along those lines. Passive resistance is the most effective method open to us. We will avoid bloodshed and the police will have no reason to use force.

Q: *Dr Moroka, many people consider that J B Marks is your most likely successor as President-General. Do you think that the fact that he is an ex-communist is any cause for concern?*

A: J B Marks is a very important member of the Congress, and I maintain that if I got out he would get in. There is no cause for concern; the fact that he is an ex-communist is not important. Of necessity, we don't believe our freedom will come from England or America. It will come from ourselves.

Some of the delegates at the 1951 annual conference in Bloemfontein. From left to right: James Phillips, Yusuf Cachalia, ANC President Dr Moroka. Front row: Manilal Gandhi, Chief Albert Luthuli, Rev V B Tantsi, ANC treasurer, Dr S Molema.

Dr Moroka was the grandson of Chief Moroka of Thaba'Nchu who, after the battle of Vegkop, had given aid and assistance to the Voortrekkers

January 1952: Dr Moroka issued the ultimatum to the Prime Minister, Dr Daniel Malan, calling for the repeal of the six unjust laws.

'We Afrikaners are not the work of man, but a creation of God. It is to us that millions of semi-barbarous blacks look for guidance, justice and the Christian way of life'

Photographs by Jurgen Schadeberg

Dr Malan states: 'The government has no intention of repealing the long-existing laws between Europeans and Bantu.'

The story of defiance

Drum: October 1952 On 6 April 1952, exactly 300 years after Van Riebeeck and the first white settlers landed at the Cape, the first mass demonstrations were held in Red Square, Fordsburg, Johannesburg (now called Freedom Square), and the other main centres of the Union. Units marched into Freedom Square from the locations and outlying towns. The meeting was addressed by the ANC and SAIC presidents, Dr Moroka and Dr Dadoo, and many other African, Indian and coloured leaders. They protested against the 'oppressive measures' and called for 10 000 volunteers to defy the laws.

The date fixed for the first defiance of the laws was 26 June, commemorating the protest strike by non-whites two years ago against living conditions. But the first actual cases of defiance, as it happened, occurred before that. On 10 May the government, under the Suppression of Communism Act, called on four 'named' non-white ex-communists to resign from all organisations: Dadoo, Marks, Bopape and Kotane. All four leaders were closely involved in the Defiance Campaign, and both Dadoo and Marks were members of the original Joint Planning Council.

The four leaders defied the order from the Minister of Justice, and continued to address meetings. With others, they were each in turn arrested. On 9 June the 'named' non-white leaders who had defied the ban came before the Magistrate's Court in Johannesburg. The week of the trial – or 'Leaders Week', as it was called – was the occasion for more protest, with crowds squeezing in and around the courts, and volunteers signing on in hundreds. All over the Union, in the towns and in the locations, the leaders made speeches for the campaign. The four principal banned leaders, together with the others, were found guilty. They were sentenced to between four and six months' imprisonment. They were granted leave to appeal and await a second trial.

In the meantime, volunteers were enlisted from all parts of the Union and from all the non-white groups to take part in acts of defiance. Men and women from all walks of life signed on, to be later organised into batches to defy the laws together.

On 26 June bands of volunteers went into action for the first time. Without violence or disorder, a small group

'No violence, no resistance to arrest,
Nkosi Sikelele Afrika!'
Leaders call for 10 000 volunteers

led by Nana Sita, an old-stager of passive resistance, insisted on entering Boksburg location, close to Johannesburg, without the necessary permits. After arguments with the police, they were arrested and, without resistance, entered the police lorry which took them to gaol. The first group was shortly followed by others, and Walter Sisulu, Secretary-General of the ANC, was one of the leaders arrested.

On the same evening a meeting was held at the Garment Workers' Hall in Anderson Street, Johannesburg. After the meeting, attended by picked bands of volunteers and a number of pressmen, a group of Africans left the building after the official curfew time. They came into the street to find a row of armed police lining the street on both sides. After brief questioning by the police chief, the group was arrested and, singing 'Afrika' and with thumbs uplifted to the 'Afrika' sign, they climbed into the waiting lorry. With them to the gaol went defiance leaders Yusuf Cachalia and Nelson Mandela.

The first groups of Defiers came up before the magistrate and were sentenced to periods from four to six weeks, with option of a fine. The fine was refused, and the Defiers served their full sentences. This was the pattern of all the defiance groups which followed. There was no violence, no resistance to arrest. The groups marched off and were taken to the gaol without incident. □

Henry Nxumalo

6 April: At Freedom Square, Fordsburg, the crowd masses to hear Moroka and Dadoo speak from the platform calling for volunteers for the campaign. 'I am glad to see you in such large numbers . . .' says Moroka.

African, coloured and Indian leaders address the crowds in Freedom Square

Mrs Viola Hashe, trade unionist leader.

James Phillips, Chairman of No 2 branch of the Garment Workers' Union.

Dr Yusuf Dadoo, President of the South African Indian Congress.

Harrison Motlana, Secretary of the Congress Youth League.

'To you who are young and whose blood is hot, we say catch the bull by its horns, Afrika!'
said one Youth League leader

Photographs by Jurgen Schadeberg

The crowd in Freedom Square makes its demands clear.

'We shall flood all the gaols in the country,' said Yusuf Cachalia

Units from all over the Reef marched into Freedom Square to protest against the unjust laws.

'This is the hour now. I am being crucified and feel the weight of the cross,' said J B Marks in a speech in anticipation of his arrest

Photographs by Jurgen Schadeberg

Yusuf Cachalia, Walter Sisulu and Dr Moroka join in the singing of 'Nkosi Sikelele Afrika', making the thumbs-up 'Afrika salute' of the Congress.

There were days during the Defiance Campaign when only women defied

26 August, Indian and African women defy the permit regulations in Germiston township and get stopped by the police.
Lower left, on crutches, Mrs Aletta Nonyane. Lower right, confronting the police, Mrs Amina Cachalia, wife of Yusuf Cachalia.

Photographs by Jurgen Schadeberg

The arrested women singing and dancing while queuing to go into the Germiston police station. Facing the camera (left) is Mrs Thoko 'Virginia' Ngomo from Alexandra.

For their defiance, these women spent two weeks in gaol. And so it goes on . . .

Photographs by Jurgen Schadeberg

Manilal Gandhi, son of the Mahatma, and Patrick Duncan, son of the wartime Governor-General Sir Patrick Duncan, join others in defying the permit regulations in a Germiston township. Left, behind Gandhi, is youth leader Moosa Mulla.

Peter Abrahams wrote: 'Undoubtedly the most important new event since I left the Union was the decision of Patrick Duncan . . . and a handful of other whites to join the Campaign of Defiance. I wonder if even they know how profoundly important their gesture of identification is? By their courage they have helped to push back the possibility of a straight clash of colour. If others join them, there may yet be hope for the whites in South Africa'

'We defy'

10 000 volunteers protest against 'unjust laws'
Here Drum *publishes a statement of the Campaign's aims*

By Nelson Mandela

Drum: August 1952 Our Defiance of Unjust Laws Campaign began on 26 June. It is going smoothly and according to plan; though there have been minor setbacks, like the arrest of Y Cachalia, SAIC General Secretary, and myself, which was not according to plan.

The support we have received from the masses has been most encouraging. At the moment, for security reasons, I cannot disclose how they are helping the Joint Planning Organisation and its sub-committees to care for the dependants of those volunteers already arrested.

I would like to emphasise the aims of our Campaign over again. We are not in opposition to any government or class of people. We are opposing a system which has for years kept a vast section of the non-European people in bondage. Though it takes us years, we are prepared to continue the Campaign until the six unjust laws we have chosen for the present phase are done away with. Even then we shall not stop. The struggle for the freedom and national independence of the non-European peoples shall continue as the National Planning Council sees fit.

As I say, we are not opposing a certain class or classes of the inhabitants of South Africa. We welcome true-hearted volunteers from all walks of life without consideration of colour, race or creed. Europeans can also join our ranks to defy these unjust laws – some of which are as unjust to them as they are to us. At the moment the Campaign is still in its first stage: defiance in Johannesburg and Port Elizabeth. Soon – perhaps even before you read this – it will move onto the next stage, which will be defiance of the laws in all the big centres of the Union. And then lastly it will assume a mass character with defiance spread all over the country; in towns as well as on the platteland.

We have sufficient volunteers for the present stage. Ever since the arrest of Kotane, Dadoo and the others who defied the Suppression of Communism Act, there has been a sudden upsurge in the rush to volunteer. It reached its peak the week following the beginning of the Campaign on 26 June.

This training has already shown its necessity, and the spirit of the volunteers is very high. This was clearly illustrated at Boksburg location when the location authorities slammed the gates closed and prevented the volunteers from entering. The volunteers waited outside the gates for a period of almost two hours until the African volunteers were arrested for pass violations. Soon thereafter, when the gates were opened, the Indian volunteers entered the location peacefully and defied the permit regulations. They were also arrested. The unity between the Africans, Indians and coloured people has now become a living reality. Volunteers are not committed to actions that will lead them behind bars. Many of them are being trained for behind-the-scenes work that is necessary for the smooth running of our plans. Theirs is as important a task as that of their comrades now behind bars.

26 August: Twenty leaders appear in court charged with contravening the Suppression of Communism Act

Fourteen of the twenty leaders on trial. Front row: B Desai, J Phillips, N Thandray, D Tloome, N Sita and M Cachalia. Back row: Y Cachalia, M Kotane, D Bopape, H Motlana, Y Dadoo, J B Marks, N Kathrada and Dr Moroka.

Photographs by Jurgen Schadeberg

People attended the trial in their thousands to show their support.

Drum: October 1952 A month after the acts of defiance had begun, on 30 July the police made sudden surprise raids on Congress offices. Searching for evidence of communist connections to the campaign, they entered the Johannesburg offices of the ANC and – after a 24-hour wait for the keys – of the SAIC offices. They also entered the homes of several leaders, including Dr Moroka's house at Thaba'Nchu in the Orange Free State. They collected a large mass of correspondence and documents for inspection.

As a result, three weeks later, warrants were issued for the arrest, under the Suppression of Communism Act, of twenty non-white leaders involved in the campaign, including Moroka, Sisulu, Marks, Mandela, Bopape, Tloome and Phillips of the ANC, and Dadoo, Thandray, Kathrada, Sita, Desai and the Cachalias of the SAIC. They were arrested and let out on bail. On 26 August the twenty leaders appeared at the Johannesburg Magistrate's Court on a charge of contravening the Suppression of Communism Act.

In the meantime, the centre of the Defiance Campaign had shifted for the first time to the Cape Province, where, in Port Elizabeth, groups of volunteers in their hundreds were defying apartheid regulations in stations and elsewhere. On 24 August the Joint Executives of the ANC had met again and advocated intensified action to coincide with the beginning of the trial of the twenty leaders. In the next 48 hours 461 people defied the law in Johannesburg, Port Elizabeth and Cape Town, and were arrested. And so the Campaign continued, and still goes on. In increasing numbers, and in spite of longer sentences and caning, defiers continue to oppose the law in all parts of the Union. Where and when will it end? □

The crowd of hundreds assembled outside the courts included 800 Indian schoolchildren making the 'Afrika' salute, on 26 August.

People sang and shouted outside the courtroom, and were only quietened when Moroka, at the request of the Court, came out and asked them to be silent and disperse

Photographs by Jurgen Schadeberg

'Be quiet my people and go in peace!' Dr Moroka says to the crowd that packed the court corridors during the first morning session of the twenty leaders' preparatory examination. After cheering, the crowd filed quietly out to an empty plot near the courts and held meetings for the rest of the day.

ANC President, Dr Moroka; National Volunteer-in-Chief, Nelson Mandela and SAIC President, Dr Yusuf Dadoo, outside the courtroom.

New laws, new threats, new punishments – especially flogging and draconian prison sentences – put an end to the Campaign

Photographs by Jurgen Schadeberg

Trialists James Phillips (left), D W Bopape, J B Marks and Walter Sisulu (left to right) chat outside the courtroom. Trialist Yusuf Dadoo and active ANC member Ruth First are in the back on right.

The Defiance Campaign trial ended with a verdict of guilty but the leaders were given suspended sentences of nine months. Judge Rumpff commented that the charge had 'nothing to do with communism as it is commonly known'

In 1952 Oliver Tambo and Nelson Mandela opened the first black law practice in Johannesburg. Both were founding members of the Congress Youth League

'Mandela and Tambo' was written huge across the frosted window panes on the second floor, and the letters stood out like a challenge. To white South Africa it was bad enough that two men with black skins should practise as lawyers, but it was indescribably worse that the letters also spelt out their political partnership

Photographs by Jurgen Schadeberg

Peter Abrahams returns to Goli

Drum: July 1952 The world-famous Johannesburg-born coloured writer, Peter Abrahams, visited the Union recently after a 14-year absence. Here he writes about a gathering arranged for him to meet various political figures, including Nelson Mandela, Walter Sisulu, and Dan Tloome, ANC organiser and Secretary of the Garment Workers' Union. The meeting was held at the Doornfontein home of James Phillips' Scottish mother.

I raised the question of coloured attitudes with them. Thuynsma, a doctor, told a story that had all the elements of a human tragedy in it. He had known a coloured man who had been white nearly all his life, who had fought in the last war as a white officer, who had had a world of white friends – and then became a coloured man quite suddenly. With precise, clinical coldness, he painted a picture of a man lost, without bearing, who had, in the middle of his life, to readjust himself to being a non-European. Such a man would naturally resent his new status. He would try to keep away from coloureds but would be isolated by whites, until, in the end, he would be forced, out of sheer need, to associate with those his whole past has made him look down on.

From there it was natural to turn to the 'marginal' position of the obviously coloured. It was agreed there are still sharp prejudices. I was told the story of the young African intellectual who has a coloured girl friend. Whenever they go to the non-European cinema they are segregated from each other. The responsibility for this must fall squarely on the Indians who own the cinema and the coloureds who endorse this apartheid among the non-whites themselves. The SAIC's Yusuf Cachalia and N Thandray have recently made personal trips around the cinemas to break down this apartheid. This is long overdue, for there can be no real unity while the oppressed adopt the same social attitude they protest against.

There is a new move towards unity among the non-Europeans. This is being spearheaded by the ANC and the SAIC. But within these two bodies there are still reservoirs of very sharp prejudice. There is, then, platform unity between the two Congresses and a degree of social apartheid on personal relations. . . For myself, I would say the day of unity has arrived when coloureds and Indians have enough faith in the Africans and their capacity for leadership to join, as individuals, the ANC and make that the one organisation for all non-Europeans. It would then be both national and African. Or are there non-Europeans who object to being called African? □

Born in coloured Albertville, Peter Abrahams, journalist and author, was by 1952 already well known for his books Wild Conquest *and* Path of Thunder. *The following year he published* Return to Goli, *about his visit to Johannesburg.*

R V Selope Thema, Editor of the Bantu World *and leader of what he called the 'national-minded block of the ANC'. On the subject of this rift in the ANC, Abrahams wrote: 'In the interest of pure fact it should be stated that Thema has hardly any following. He has, of course, the* Bantu World, *and a man with a paper can always start a political party if he is so minded.'*

Photographs by Jurgen Schadeberg

Dr J Thuynsma, a medicine-man (European-style) with a very didactic manner. Back right, Nelson Mandela, described by Abrahams as a 'coldly reserved and brilliant young man'.

Trade unionist James Phillips. He was a member of the South African Communist Party. James had an outstanding bass voice which dominated all other voices when singing freedom songs.

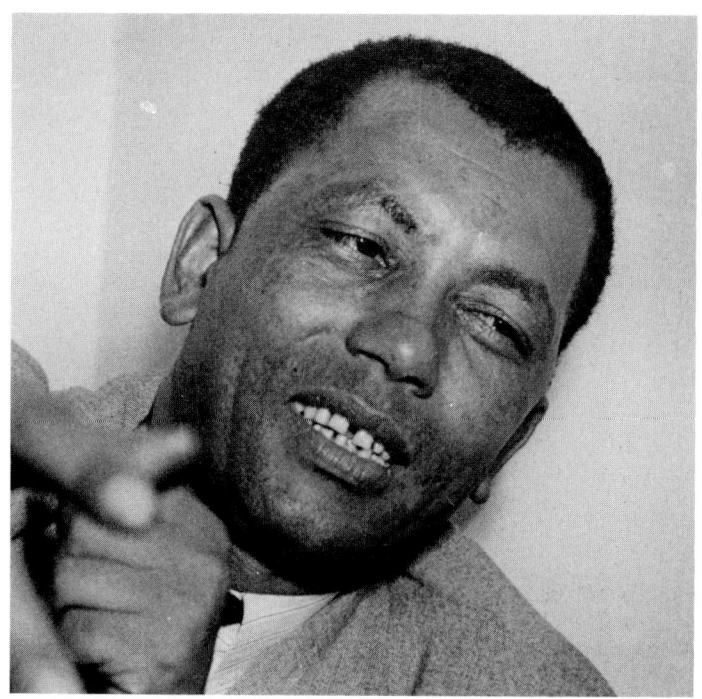

Walter Sisulu, ANC Secretary-General: 'Africanism is the basis of our struggle'. Sisulu served on the Joint Planning Council for the Defiance Campaign and led one of the first batches of passive resisters.

Henry 'Mr Drum' Nxumalo, journalist and old friend of Peter Abrahams. They had met in England during the war when Henry was in the army.

Chief Albert Luthuli – the new ANC President

Photographs by G R Naidoo

Dr Moroka, after handing over the presidency of the ANC to Chief Luthuli. During the Defiance Campaign trial, Dr Moroka had arranged his own private defence, independently of the other trialists, and had consequently fallen from favour within the ANC.

In 1951 Chief Albert Luthuli entered politics almost by accident, when he attended a meeting at which the successor of the Natal ANC leader, A W G Champion, was to be elected. The meeting had bogged down in confusion when Luthuli suddenly leapt onto the platform and called for order. Luthuli was promptly elected the new Natal ANC President. A year later, in December 1952, Chief Luthuli became the President of the ANC

Interview with Luthuli!

Drum: May 1953

Q: *Do you think there is hope for South Africa?*

A: Yes, I do. But a bitter conflict can only be avoided if those in power can adjust their thinking to accept the sharing of power with others. Otherwise there will be no real peace in this country. I firmly believe that the different races can live together amicably, but first they must abandon selfishness and fear. Most of the difficulties that the Europeans are now facing are the result of selfishness. We are like members of a family who cannot live together if they are selfish or jealous of one another.

Q: *Will your presidency mark a change in Congress policy?*

A: No. Our elections are not party elections, and the power for making decisions lies not in the President alone but in the National Executive. I have not the right or the means to make the Congress conform to my personal views.

In his office and on Durban's Esplanade, the President of the Congress gives his views to Drum *in this important interview with Anthony Sampson*

Q: *Do you consider that communism is a serious menace to South Africa?*

A: No, I do not. The nature of our own movement at present is nationalist rather than communist. There should be room for all political parties among us. At the moment we are concerned only with rescuing ourselves out of the mire, and we cannot yet say which direction we shall follow after that. For myself, I would wish for socialism, in the British sense – if I were in England I would vote for Attlee. But in the Congress we have people of many different political beliefs; capitalists, socialists, and the rest . . .

Q: *Is there a danger of extreme nationalism in the Congress?*

A: There is no sign of it at present, and the fact that we have welcomed co-operation with other races shows that it is being avoided. We recognise the danger and are guarding against it.

Q: *Will the policy of the Congress be affected by the party in power?*

A: No. As the Nationalists themselves have said, the laws which we oppose were not passed by them alone. One which we consider most unjust, for instance, the Land Act of 1913, was passed by the South African Party, from which the United Party has evolved over the years.

Q: *Do you think that there is a common cause between Indians and Africans?*

A: Yes. Our immediate objects are bound to be the same, and we can and must work closely together. Since we welcome the sympathy and support of all races in the rest of the world, it would be absurd and contradictory to reject Indians in our own country. I myself would rather see the African people utterly destroyed than see them turn against the Indians.

Q: *Can the Congress claim to be truly representative?*

A: Yes. We genuinely represent organised African opinion in this country, and we are not influenced by any single clique. The fact that the last three presidents have been in turn Xhosa, Basuto and Zulu, shows that there has been no tribal bias.

Q: *Are Africans still prepared to accept leadership from the whites?*

A: Since the 1936 Hertzog bills, the African peoples have lost faith in the good intentions of the whites to improve their conditions and the Congress movement has become more and more a liberatory one. It is no longer possible for an African leader to appeal for better conditions only; what the people demand is political rights. By joining the Natives' Representative Council, the African leaders gave the whites a last chance to prove their good faith, but they have not done so. □

OLD STAGERS

DR. ALFRED XUMA, ex - President; dapper and thoughtful; moderate and clear-headed.

RICHARD G. BALOYI, ex-Treasurer; business man; long-winded but firm

A. G. CHAMPION, ex-Natal President, ex-I.C.U. veteran; parochial nationalist.

HIGH-UPS

PROFESSOR Z. K. MATTHEWS, Cape President; brilliant debater, conservative; Fort Hare professor.

DR. SILAS MOLEMA, Treasurer; Mafeking medico, farmer, dealer and postal agent; scholarly writer.

DR. WILSON CONCO, Natal Deputy - President; thoughtful future hope, reserved; ex-Wits student.

DR. WILFRED NKOMO, Pretoria executive; outspoken rational, controversial successful and musical

WHO'S WHO IN CONGRESS

IN the last few months considerable changes have occurred in the African National Congress. Notices have been served on many leaders in terms of the Riotous Assemblies act, forbidding them to enter various districts, and from attending any sort of public meeting. Other leaders have been convicted of being "statutory" communists under the Suppression of Communism Act, and are under a suspended sentence of nine months imprisonment. The appeal by twenty leaders against this judgment was rejected two months ago.

At the same time elections have been held in the different provinces, and various changes have been made in the leadership.

For these and other reasons new faces have appeared, and new people have come to the forefront of African politics. On these two pages DRUM reviews some of the personalities in Congress today, excluding all those who have been convicted at the time of writing.

In collaboration with the Church of England and various European organisations, Congress is now engaged in protesting against the removal of 75,000 non-Europeans from the Western Areas of Johannesburg to an area fifteen miles south of the city. A private meeting at Sophiatown's Odin Cinema on Sunday, June 28, was held to protest against the removal, and 1,000 delegates from the

NATIONAL-MINDED CRITICS

E. P. MORETSELE, executive member; self-made patriot; steady and sincere.

J. G. MTWESI, National Bloc's chief protagonist; fire-eating speaker; soft goods salesman.

R. V. SELOPE-THEMA, Bloc President and retired journalist; first Secretary of Congress; nationalist.

M. P. NHLABATHI, Bloc enthusiast; runs Swazi Mercantile Company; leading Swazi on Rand.

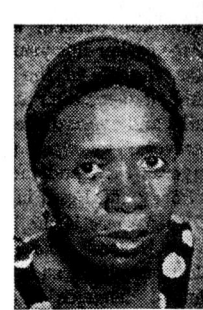

MISS L. TSHABALALA, Chairman of Zululand Daughters one of Bloc's only two women.

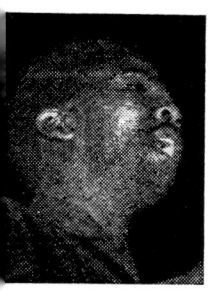

ROBERT RESHA, Youth League President; journalist and law clerk; short, self-made, husky voiced.

different districts of the Western Areas attended.

At the meeting, which was opened by the Rev. Father Huddleston, C.R., Mr. Yusuf Cachalia, Secretary of the Transvaal Indian Congress, was arrested and later released on £15 bail.

The African National Congress continues to work closely in co-operation with the South African Indian Congress. In opposition to this policy is the "national-minded bloc," under the leadership of R. V. Selope-Thema, who advocate a purely African Congress, excluding Coloureds within Congress and advocating apartheid between the non-European races.

Other opponents of Congress policy include the Bantu National Congress, led by S. S. Benghu, in Natal (see Page 37) and the Left-wing Unity Movement, centred on Cape Town and led largely by Coloured teachers and intellectuals.

PRESIDENT OF CONGRESS

ALBERT J. LUTHULI, 55-year-old farmer, is A.N.C.'s eighth president. He is at present banned from attending any public gathering and from visiting 21 magisterial districts. Son of an American Board Church missionary, Luthuli is himself a devout Christian. He has toured America and represented the African Christian Council at the last Tambaran (Indian) World Conference of Churches. He left teaching at Adams College, Natal, to become chief of the Maqadini tribe and was deposed last year for his political activities.

BACK ROOM BOYS

PETER MDA, second Y.L. President after Lembede; now sickly; aspires to law; strong nationalist.

JORDAN K. NGUBANE, political analyst, journalist, poultry farmer; influential Natal lobbyist.

OLIVER TAMBO, solicitor and Youth League foundation member; polite and powerful speaker.

BANNED MEN

M. B. YENGWA, Natal Secretary; successful business man and company secretary; ex-Natal University student.

JOE MATTHEWS, Youth League Secretary; teacher, law student and Z.K.'s son; bearded uncompromising Cape stalwart.

ROBERT MATJI, Cape Secretary; ex-Pretoria trade unionist and ex-wine steward; fast speaking and impatient.

REV. N. B. TANTSI, Transvaal's acting President and chaplain; amicable; Pretoria A.M.E. minister.

MISS IDA MNTWANA, Youth Leaguer; moving spirit among women; orator and heckler.

Something everyone wants at the price everyone can afford!

Scroll STAR BALL PENS — 4/9

REFILLS TOO... The SCROLL long-life refills are now on sale at stationers, stores everywhere. A new one is fitted in a few seconds!

Trade Enquiries: CENTRAL NEWS AGENCY LTD.

FORUM

A monthly magazine for readers of intelligence and discernment

Annual Subscription 13s.
Rhodesias - 14s.
Overseas - 15s.

P.O. Box 1067, Johannesburg

Be a Master of English

Improve Your Speech and Writing in a Few Hours

You are judged by the way you speak and write.

Improve your English quickly by post—the Regent way. Many students say that the moderate fee charged for the Effective English course is the best investment they have ever made.

The tuition is so planned that you make noticeable progress within a few hours. Confirm this by taking advantage of the special offer now available.

Send a postal order for one shilling to The Regent Institute (Dept. 555), Palace Gate, London, W.8, England, for specimen lesson and "Word Mastery" (the prospectus). This valuable offer is made so that you may satisfy yourself that the Course is what you require.

Don't delay. Accept this offer NOW. Your English is all-important to you, and you cannot afford to neglect it.

Who's Who INDIAN

BIG SHOTS

DR. G. M. NAICKER, Natal president; banned from public meetings; SAIC president till 1950; formed Congress against late A. I. Kajee.

YUSUF CACHALIA, SAIC joint secretary; banned from public meetings; ex-soft goods salesman; energetic; eloquent, dramatic.

MAULVI CACHALIA, Transvaal joint secretary; brilliant, well-read Moslem priest; brother of Yusuf; Congress's legal brain.

MONEYBAGS

GOOLUM PAHAD, soft goods salesman; clear thinker; wife Amina is on Women's Action Committee; hard-working; hospitable.

D. U. MISTRY (42), Hindu; joint secretary of SAIC; wealthy and leisured Johannesburg attorney; dignified political old-stager.

DR. M. PADYACHEE, Natal Congress treasurer; hospitable and pleasant personality; Dr. Naicker's bosom pal; fund raiser.

TWO of the most important branches of the South African Indian Congress were formed long before Union. The Natal Indian Congress was formed by Mahatma Gandhi in 1893, and nine years later Gandhi formed the Transvaal British Association to protect the interests of Transvaal Indians.

Gandhi organised passive resistance to laws affecting Indians as far back as 1906-14, resulting in an agreement reached between Gandhi and Smuts; but further restrictions on Indians owning land were introduced in 1919, and opposition to this led to the formation of a national organisation, the South African Indian Congress, with the Cape Independent Council representing Cape Indians.

Agitation increased after further laws had been passed. But certain differences occurred in the internal affairs of the Transvaal in 1927 and the Transvaal British Association seceded from the SAIC; the Transvaal Indian Congress was then formed to replace it as a constituent body of the SAIC.

Dr. Dadoo came back to South Africa from Europe in 1936 and began to take part in politics. In 1938 he introduced a more militant line of struggle

YOUNG BLOOD

ACHIE E. PATEL, cinema proprietor; devoted Congress worker for past 10 years; but thrives in spite of it; Transvaal executive.

CASSIM AMRA, Natal Congress executive trade unionist; good debater; thrown out of Cape Town University for his political

M. P. NAICKER, energetic Natal organising secretary; ex - market vendor and working-class leader, full-time. SAIC representative.

S. M. RAHIM, Cape Indian Assembly president; fez-wearing but 20th - century - minded; most outstanding Indian in Cape politics.

T. N. NAIDOO (40), Transvaal vice-president; heart - troubled and hard of hearing; upright, indomitable; Gandhi's adopted son.

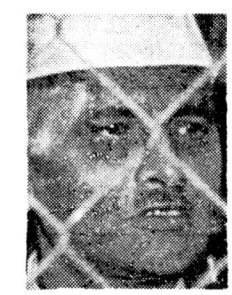

NANA SITA, Transvaal's ailing president; rheumatic; emotional speaker and Gandhi exponent; Pretoria shopkeeper.

J. N. SINGH (34), Natal general secretary; ex-Wits.; solicitor; SAIC representative; pleasant, convincing debater; popular.

SALOOJEE (22), Johannesburg Central South Congress secretary; active; lives Congress; doesn't like police and they ditto.

MOOSA MOOLA (17), Youth Congress joint secretary; devil-may-care speaker; expelled from high school for taking part in politics.

DR. HASSIM MOOSA, dapper; chairman, Indian Youth Congress; ex - C.T.U. politician; wife, Rahima, is prominent trades unionist.

in the CONGRESS

into the Transvaal Indian Congress and co-operation and unity among the non-Europeans.

The SAIC itself remained modest and cautious in its demands, but by 1945 this policy was not acceptable to Dr. Naicker, the Natal president, and Dr. Dadoo, the Transvaal president. The two leaders set about planning a more radical policy; and in 1946 the Transvaal Indian Youth Congress was formed as an offshoot of the mother body. Dr. Naicker became SAIC president in 1949, and was succeeded by Dr. Dadoo in 1950. In recent months several leaders, including Dadoo, Naicker and Yusuf Cachalia, have been temporarily banned from attending public meetings.

The constitution of the SAIC aims to improve the relations between Indians and whites and to promote friendship between all South Africans. It seeks to achieve its aims by legitimate means for the interests of South African Indians and to help other communities.

Since the Dadoo-Naicker leadership took over in the SAIC they have implemented the policy of bringing about closer co-operation and unity between Africans, Coloureds and Indians.

From Clerk to Bank Accountant thanks to THE FAMOUS BENNETT COLLEGE

ENGLISH QUALIFICATIONS HELPED THIS YOUNG MAN TO SUCCESS

This is the success story of a young man, who although he was only a clerk with a very small salary, was determined to get ahead. That is why he wrote to the Governor of The Famous Bennett College, in England, asking for advice on a career in accountancy. After reading the college prospectus, which he received by return of post, he enrolled immediately.

Shortly after he had completed his course, he wrote to tell us that he had taken his Royal Society of Arts Examination and had passed it with honours — First Class in Commerce, Second Class in Book-keeping and Accountancy. He is now an Accountant in a great bank — at a much increased salary.

In a letter* to the Governor of The Bennett College he thanked him for his "fatherly guidance in my studies and the close co-operation of your expert tutors which have contributed to my progress in life".

When you take a course with The Bennett College, you are taught from England through personal, postal tuition. This means that you work in your own time and at your own pace.

All the text books that you need are provided free. The Bennett College *guarantees* to teach you until you have *qualified* for the diploma or exam for which you entered.

Some of the subjects in which you can get ENGLISH QUALIFICATIONS

Accountancy Exams. Auditing. Book-keeping. Commercial Arithmetic. Modern Business Methods. Shorthand. English. General Education Languages. Mathematics. Police Subjects. Secretarial Exams. Architecture. Agriculture. Building. Carpentry. Chemistry. Civil Engineering. Diesel Engines. Draughtsmanship Electrical Engineering. Electrical Instruments. Electric Wiring. Engineering Drawings. Locomotive Eng. Machine Design. Mechanical Engineering. Motor Engineering. Plumbing. Press Tool Work. Quantity Surveying. Radio Engineering. Road Making. Sanitation Sheet Metal Work. Surveying. Telecommunications. Television Wireless Telegraphy. Workshop Practice.

OVERSEAS SCHOOL CERTIFICATE. GENERAL CERT OF EDUCATION. R.S.A EXAMS.

SEND THIS COUPON TODAY

To The FAMOUS BENNETT COLLEGE, Department 330, Sheffield, England.

Please send me your prospectus on _____ subject
NAME _____
ADDRESS _____
AGE (if under 21) _____
PLEASE WRITE IN BLOCK LETTERS

FEES ARE EXTREMELY LOW. You can join for as little as 30/- followed by monthly instalments of 15/- until the total fee is paid.

*The letter may be seen in The Bennett College's files in Sheffield, England

---

WHOLESALE BARGAIN STORES LTD.
KIRKDALE ROAD, SOUTH WIGSTON LEICESTER, ENGLAND

Offer you these
Wonderful Bargains in Superb Quality
AMERICAN STYLE SHOES
MADE IN ENGLAND

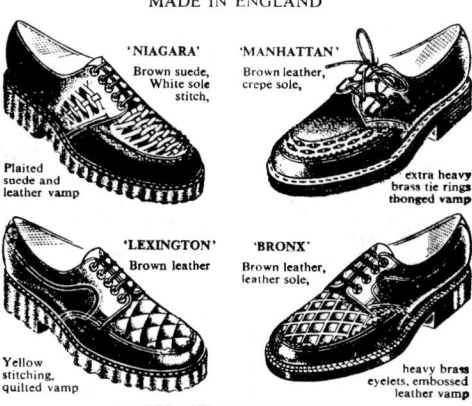

'NIAGARA' Brown suede, White sole stitch. Plaited suede and leather vamp

'MANHATTAN' Brown leather, crepe sole, extra heavy brass tie rings thonged vamp

'LEXINGTON' Brown leather. Yellow stitching, quilted vamp

'BRONX' Brown leather, leather sole, heavy brass eyelets, embossed leather vamp

IN FULL AND HALF SIZES 6 TO 11

EVERY PAIR GUARANTEED **45/-** DESPATCHED IMMEDIATELY

Just send a postal order for 45/- with your order

Important to Shopkeepers — THERE IS GOOD BUSINESS HERE

Orders of 25 pairs or over are subject to a special sales commission

All you have to do is to take the orders and cash Write to our Export Department at the above address

June 1953

Western Areas protest meeting

ANC Secretary-General, Walter Sisulu, addressing the meeting.

Sunday, 28 June 1953: The ANC and Transvaal Indian Congress convened a public meeting at Sophiatown's Odin Cinema to protest against government plans to demolish Johannesburg's Western Areas townships – Sophiatown, Newclare and Martindale – and to move their African residents to Meadowlands, a new State township

Photographs by Jurgen Schadeberg

Father Trevor Huddleston opens the meeting, which was attended by at least 1 000 Western Areas delegates.

The Special Branch arrests one of the main speakers, Yusuf Cachalia. Father Huddleston (right) protests.

Cachalia is taken away. He was arrested for addressing a gathering in defiance of his banning order.

Head of the Special Branch, Major Spengler (middle), Father Huddleston and Yusuf Cachalia (far right) outside the cinema, where the argument about the arrest continued.

Drum: November 1953

Political football

Dr Yusuf Dadoo, playing (of course) at Veterans' inside left, treated the ball very gingerly. His play was described as 'cautious'.

Tough centre forward, Baragwanath doctor, Diliza Mji, prepares to take a header, while spectators look on expectantly. Brawny Mji led the Veterans to victory.

'Foul play!' complains left back, Moses Kotane (holding the ball): he protests that Youth player Babla Salojee kicked the ball while it was in the goalie's hands. Referee Dan Twala reprimands him.

'The most remarkable game I've ever seen,' was referee Dan Twala's comment on the match between Congress Veterans and Youth.

Non-white political leaders, banned from doing much else, enjoy a lively game of soccer at Mia's farm, near Johannesburg

Photographs by Bob Gosani

There was some surprise at Oliver Tambo (above) playing left wing, both from political and sports observers, but Molvi Cachalia played an excellent game at right wing, and Dadoo and Kotane were very comfortable at inside left and left back. Veterans, of course, won 1-0 after half an hour's devastating play.

December 1953

The ANC holds its annual congress in Queenstown

Chief Albert Luthuli, ANC President-General, gives the 'Afrika' salute to delegates at the conference.

At the 41st annual congress held in Queenstown, Cape, three hundred delegates from every part of the Union came to give their views, pass resolutions and discuss a scheme for economic boycott. The conference was said to have been the biggest in the history of the Congress

Photographs by Bob Gosani

'We can assure the world that it is our intention to keep on the non-violent plane,' said Chief Luthuli in his presidential address. From left are *Duma Nokwe, Chief Luthuli, the Rev Calata, Oliver Tambo and Walter Sisulu.*

Duma Nokwe, Chief Luthuli, Rev James Calata, Oliver Tambo and Walter Sisulu on the dais singing 'Nkosi Sikelele Afrika' during the three-day conference.

ANC Executive members on the platform at the annual conference listening to views from the floor. Left Philip Vundla, Duma Nokwe, Professor Matthews, Rev James Calata (rosette) and Walter Sisulu (right, with glasses).

Photographs by Bob Gosani

'One of the old troubles of Africans was racialism – but your meeting has killed that,' said the Rev Ngqoqa of Queenstown, welcoming delegates to the Cape.

'We base our struggle on a spiritual foundation,' said Professor Z K Matthews, Speaker of the Conference. 'We are struggling against spiritual wickedness . . .'

'Women have been used as tools to raise money, without representation in the Congress,' strongly protested Mrs Gelana Twala, delegate for Alexandra township.

'We must see ourselves as messengers of Christ, not apologising for the colour God gave us . . .' said the Rev Walter Gawe of Queenstown, in opening the conference.

69

Z K: Africa's leading 'Ambassador' returns

Photograph by Bob Gosani

Professor Z K Matthews, the son of a Kimberley diamond miner and café owner, is one of only two black professors in South Africa. He is also Cape President of the ANC, a position he has held since 1949. He joined the organisation in 1942. He has just returned from America where he has been lecturing at New York's Union Theological Seminary

Drum interviews the Cape President of the African National Congress, Professor Z K Matthews, who has lately returned from America

Drum: April 1954

Drum: *From your visit to America, did you feel that the people there were sympathetic with Africans in South Africa?*

Prof Matthews: The people are very sympathetic, including organisations such as churches, universities, trade unions, clubs, etc. But the government is much more careful and cautious. I noticed a great change from the previous time I had been in America in 1935. At that time the Negroes didn't seem at all interested in African problems. They said they were Americans, not Africans, and seemed anxious to forget their African background. But this time it was quite different. One day I was walking down 125th Street in New York, and I saw a big crowd attending a meeting. When I got near I realised that it was a meeting for African nationalism! So I joined in . . .

I was surprised too when two Negro ladies called on me one evening. They had come to complain that in my speeches I had advocated a policy of 'Africa for the Africans too': they said I should preach 'Africa for the Africans only'. They explained that they belonged to the Garvey Movement founded by Marcus Garvey in 1914, which aimed at persuading American Negroes to return to their homeland, and once actually bought ships for the purpose. I said I still thought there was room for all races in Africa.

Drum: *Are the American Negroes really becoming integrated with the whites?*

Prof Matthews: Yes, more and more. Even some of the states that have recently been opposing the opening of primary and secondary schools to Negroes, have opened their universities to Negroes. They are finding that they cannot afford 'separate but equal' institutions, even if it were possible. In Texas four years ago they built a university for Negroes only which cost twelve million dollars. Now they find they cannot afford to keep it Negro, they are admitting whites too.

There was the case of the Negro student who complained of unequal facilities in a separate law school specially created for the one man, with professors and lecturers. But even then he complained that he didn't have fellow students – so they had to admit him to a white university!

Drum: *Do you think that the Cape Province is more politically conscious than the Transvaal?*

Prof Matthews: Here in the Cape the political temper of the people is very high. In addressing political meetings round the country I have noticed people are much more awake politically than they were before the Defiance Campaign. But I am informed the temper is not so high as it was at the height of the Campaign.

In the Transvaal people are politically minded, but also tend to be more politically divided. They have more groups with different tribal backgrounds speaking different languages. But in the Eastern Cape the African people belong principally to the same language group. And at the same time in the Cape there is a much older tradition of political education.

There have been rumours around that the Cape is trying to gain leadership of the Congress and wrest power from the Transvaal and other provinces. I can assure you that we have no such designs. □

Walter Sisulu, Secretary-General of the ANC, and Yusuf Cachalia, South African Indian Congress (SAIC) Secretary, signed a statement, 'to who it may concern', on 20 January 1953, certifying that Prof Matthews was 'the accredited representative and plenipotentiary' of the ANC and SAIC in dealing with the United Nations General Assembly's fact-finding commission on South Africa

Drum: October 1954

'I like it where I am'

'Let us be true to our friends in the Western Areas,' said P Q Vundla, ANC Executive. He called for volunteers to assist in resisting the scheme.

Father Trevor Huddleston, Chairman of the Western Areas Protest Committee. 'Racialism, in any form, is an attack not only upon the nature of Man, but upon the nature of God Himself.'

Elias Moretsele, Transvaal ANC President. 'The people do not want to be removed against their will. They do not want to be herded into controlled black townships.'

Mayibuye! . . . Afrika!

Under the leadership of the ANC, residents of Sophiatown, Martindale and Newclare protested against government plans to destroy their homes and to move them to government-controlled townships like Meadowlands

Western Areas Protest Conference in Johannesburg

Photographs by Bob Gosani

'My people, be calm: don't get excited,' said Elias Moretsele, when 100 policemen entered the meeting. The police said they were investigating a charge of treason and took the names of everyone present.

Sunday, 27 June 1954, was declared a day of 'Solidarity with the Western Areas' and a 'Resist apartheid' conference was held that day at the Trades Hall, Johannesburg. It was convened by five organisations, headed by the ANC, and attended by 1 000 delegates. The conference resolved that 'the attempted uprooting of the people and the destruction of the right to own land, are the most flagrant violations of human rights and elementary decency'

What will happen in the Western Areas?

Drum: October 1954 Tension is mounting in the Western Areas of Johannesburg where 58 000 residents are due to be moved ten miles out of town to Meadowlands where 300 houses have already been built to house the first batch of evicted families. Residents, led by P Q Vundla and Robert Resha of the ANC, want to stay where they are. Meetings in different parts of the country have been called by various organisations to protest against the Western Areas move, together with the new Bantu Education Act and the Native Labour Act.

The Department of Native Affairs has announced that the first families will be moved when the first 1 000 houses are ready for occupation, which will be at the end of the year at the earliest. The department is confident that the removal will be completed without serious trouble. In the meantime, meetings of Western Areas residents continue to say: 'We won't move.' What is going to happen?

On 27 June a protest conference was held in Johannesburg. The previous day a mass meeting was held at Uitenhage in the Eastern Cape. It was addressed by Chief Albert Luthuli, President of the ANC. After the meeting Luthuli issued a press statement in which he said:

'We call the attention of the whole country to the profound racial clash which the Nationalist Government is about to provoke by the forcible removal of 60 000 people from their traditionally established homes in Johannesburg's Western Areas . . . We observe with gratification the tremendous campaign conducted by Europeans, no less than non-Europeans, to shift the government from a reckless, bloodthirsty and reactionary course. . .'

In the meantime the whole world is watching the families in the Western Areas, and the houses in Meadowlands. Will they move, or will they stay? □

Drum: February 1955 The first sixty families in Sophiatown have been given orders to leave their houses, and have been offered accommodation in Meadowlands. 'You are hereby required in terms of the Native Resettlement Act of 1954 to vacate the premises in which you reside. . .' The first date given is 12 February. Meetings have been held in all parts of the Western Areas to decide on future action. Walls have been painted with slogans, 'We won't move' and 'Hands off Newclare'.

What will happen? *Drum* interviewed Elias Moretsele, Transvaal President of the ANC, a Johannesburg businessman and resident of Western Areas. 'Feelings are running high', said Moretsele, 'most of the people simply want to sit down and refuse to leave. Property owners in Sophiatown are against being deprived of land and buildings that have cost them so much time, money and energy. Many tenants, too, realise that in Meadowlands they will be under severe restrictions. People simply don't want to be herded into camps like locations; it's against man's dignity. The Congress, as you know, believes in non-violence and will discourage violence as much as is within its power. Let those who want to provoke do so; we have progressive forces on our side. There can be no talk of defiance in this matter.'

In the meantime, some landowners in the Western Areas have already sold their properties to the government, and some tenants and landlords have already moved to Dube Village where a thirty-year lease is available. The government maintains that there is little genuine opposition to the scheme, and that accommodation at Meadowlands will be a great improvement on the overcrowded houses of Sophiatown and Vrededorp. Undoubtedly, the Western Areas Scheme is an important and significant development, and the world is watching anxiously to see what will happen. □

Sophiatown, January 1955. 'Many tenants realise that in Meadowlands they will be under severe restrictions. People simply don't want to be herded into camps like locations; it's against man's dignity.'

Photographs by Jurgen Schadeberg

Three days after the first eviction orders were sent to residents, the ANC issued a statement: 'The African people have rejected the removal scheme as a brutal and wicked plot . . . to rob the African people of freehold rights and to resettle them in specified areas in tribal groups . . . If the Nationalists implement the removal scheme, an extremely dangerous and explosive situation will arise'

The Effects of New Laws: 2

BANNED MEN

DURING the last few months, nearly all the non-White leaders in South Africa have been restricted in their movements and activities. Most of them have been called upon to resign their positions in the African National Congress or the South African Indian Congress. Many of them have been forbidden to attend any gatherings, or to enter certain magisterial districts in the Union.

Albert Luthuli, for instance, president of the African National Congress, is forbidden to move away from his own district at Groutville, Natal. He cannot visit the shops in Durban, thirty miles away, or attend the cathedral there.

Most of the bans are in force for two years, after which time they may be renewed: some have already been renewed.

The bans take effect under the Suppression of Communism Act of 1950. This allows the Minister of Justice to prohibit from gatherings or organisations anyone suspected of furthering the aims of Communism. 'Communism' is defined under the act as aiming to bring about social economic or political changes in the country.

Many of those convicted or 'named' under the Suppression of Communism Act are not 'Communists' in the usual sense of the term, but 'Statutory Communists' who come within the definition of the act.

Yusuf Dadoo, ex-president, SAIC.
Nelson Mandela, ex-president, Tvl. ANC.
James Phillips, ex-chairman, Tvl. CPAC.
Duma Nokwe, secretary, ANC Y.L.
Walter Sisulu, ex-secretary, ANC.
Albert Luthuli, president, ANC.
Yusuf Cachalia, secretary, SAIC.
John B. Marks, ex-president, Tvl. ANC.
Stephen Sello, ex-Tvl. acting secretary.
David Bopape, ex-secretary, Tvl. ANC.
Moses Kotane, ex-leader, ANC.
Dr. Z. Njongwe, ex-chairman, ANC.
Cassim Amra, ex-leader, Indian C.
Dr. Diliza Mji, ex-secretary, ANC. 
Dr. Silas M. Molema, ex-treasurer, ANC. 
Maulvi Cachalia, ex-secretary, Tvl. I.C. 
J. Mavuso, ex-Transvaal ANC leader. 
Nana Sitha, ex-president, Transvaal I.C. 
Dan Tlhoome, ex-leader, ANC. 
Flag Boshielo, ex-leader, Transvaal ANC. 
N. Thandray, ex-Tvl. secretary, I.C. 
Hosia Seperepere, ex-leader, ANC. 
Frank Marquard, ex-president, Cape F.W.U. 
Joseph Matthews, ex-president, ANC Y.L. 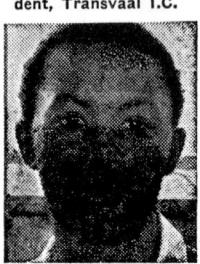
Robert Matji, ex-secretary, Cape ANC. 
MacDon. Maseko, ex-leader, ANC. 
Ismail Bhoola, ex-sec., Tvl. Indian YC. 
Harrison Motlana, ex-secretary, Tvl. Y.L.

'All the banned leaders belong to you,' declared Walter Sisulu, before he was himself banned. 'They will remain your leaders because they still belong to our liberation struggle and they will still find a way to make their contribution. They have not been rejected by us, but forcibly thrown out by our enemies'

Photograph by Gopal Naransamy

Walter Max Ulyate Sisulu was born in the Engcobo district of the Transkei. Walter left home in 1929 and his first job was in a Johannesburg dairy. Thereafter he worked as a gold miner on the Reef and later he worked in a kitchen. In 1930 he took a series of factory jobs and studied to improve his education. Sisulu joined the ANC in 1940 and became Secretary-General in 1949.

How red is the Congress?

Drum: January 1955 The Congress long ago decided that it would not discriminate against any person because of his/her other political associations. So long as a member subscribed to Congress policy, which was first of all African Unity, and secondly working for the welfare of the African people, and so long as he was an African, he would not be debarred from membership. Long before the present flare-up about communists, there have always been members of the Congress who were communists – even before the Congress adopted its militant programme. The Congress did not ally itself with communism because it had communist members, and it even took a stand against communism as such.

Recently the Congress has grown to be the spearhead of the liberatory movement. Anyone in the liberatory movement, so long as he pledges himself to work for the realisation of freedom for all people in South Africa, would be welcome. We have the Congress of Democrats (COD) now, who are part of the liberatory movement, and no doubt they have members who are ex-communists. But there are people in COD who have never been communists.

When we initiated the Defiance Campaign, the people in it were the ANC and the South African Indian Congress (SAIC). No one could honestly say that these two organisations were dominated by communists. What is more likely is that our thinking was influenced by the success of the non-violent passive resistance of the Indian National Congress of India. People who say that the Campaign for the Defiance of Unjust Laws was initiated by communists forget that communism has never embraced 'non-violence' as a basic philosophy for its struggles.

The general plan to make the Congress more militant was agreed on in 1949, under the presidency of Dr Alfred Xuma. A committee was formed at the time to study the form that militancy should take. No one in a sane mood would accuse Dr Xuma of being a communist, and the same is true of his successor, Dr Moroka, and also very true of Dr Moroka's successor, myself.

As far as Mr Sisulu's visit to Moscow is concerned, it was a personal invitation, not an invitation to the Congress; his visit was not in any way an official Congress visit. Professor Matthews also accepted a private invitation to go to America. On their return, Both Mr Sisulu and Professor Matthews gave semi-official reports to the Congress on their visits, but this does not mean that the Congress was influenced either by America or Russia. So far as I know, the Congress lays no bars to its leaders, duly invited, going to any country in the world.

I believe the Congress, in general, follows the foreign policy of Nehru: we wish to be neither East nor West but neutral; and we welcome co-operation from those on either side who will help to further our aspirations for freedom in a democratic set-up. If we get more support from the East than from the West it is not our fault. In fact, to my knowledge, we have enjoyed considerable support from the West – perhaps even more than from the East – and I am as grateful for it as I would be grateful for legitimate support from the East.

The ANC has consistently, through its presidents and other leaders, indicated that they are interested in democracy within the present framework of the Union. There is nothing to suggest that behind the Congress there are people working for Moscow. If ever I were convinced that the Congress was working for Moscow, I would definitely resign.

What in fact South Africa is hearing from the ANC is the voice of African nationalism rather than communism. In fact, our task as leaders is to make this nationalism a broad nationalism, rather than the narrow nationalism of the Nationalist Party.

Some people say that the fact that ex-communists are elected to Parliament by the Cape Western constituency shows that the Congress is influenced by communists. It does not. These candidates have won their seats because of their part in working for the people locally; in fact, this should be a lesson to white South Africa, that Africans will judge you by what you do for them, not by your ideologies.

One ex-communist in the Congress has said, 'I would quarrel with my own colleagues if they were to use the Congress platform to further communist objectives, because at present we are engaged together in a liberatory movement. When we have freedom, then might be the time to split and fight on ideological questions.' I would be much surprised if ex-communists formed as much as one per cent of the Congress membership. I can quite believe that the banning of the Communist Party has led African ex-communists in the Congress to be more active than before within the Congress programme, but this does not mean that the Congress is becoming more communist. □

Chief Albert Luthuli

Is the ANC communist-controlled? Does it represent the African people? Chief Albert Luthuli, President-General of the Congress, wrote for Drum *about these vital questions*

Photograph by Ranjith Kally

'If I were convinced that the Congress was working for Moscow I would resign'.

Parents boycott Bantu Education

Banned children mean empty desks in this class at the Ikage School, Alexandra. Three teachers have been sacked from the school.

Drum: June 1955 A black cloud is sweeping over African education today. That unfortunate Bantu Education Act has arrived! In terms of it, control of African education will be transferred from the provinces to the Bantu Education Department on 1 April, and the government will control syllabuses, pupil admission and the employment of teachers. The act also makes it a criminal offence to run a school unless it has been registered by the Department. Masses of parents, under the banner of the ANC, particularly on the Reef, went on boycott by withdrawing their children from schools.

And the government's reply? Children who did not turn up for school by 25 April would be banned from further schooling anywhere in the Union. In the Western Areas, 1 000 parents decided to send their children back before the deadline and a prominent local ANC leader, P Q Vundla, supported their decision. (For this, youth leaders beat him up and the ANC expelled him.) Many others though, continued their boycott and altogether 6 948 pupils have been banned from school. As a result, the Education Department has given 116 teachers a month's notice to leave school. The school-going population outside school has thus been increased immensely. Banned pupils, sacked teachers, half-empty schools!

Of all the schools on the Reef, those in Brakpan, where 1 300 pupils have been expelled, have been hit hardest by the dismissal of teachers: at the Central Senior and Junior schools, 15 out of 27 teachers have been dismissed. The Newclare Community School lost 9 out of 11, and the Western Areas as a whole, where 2 000 pupils are boycotting, lost 70.

What is going to happen to these children who are not allowed to go back to school? This question is worrying many people, not least the ANC, which has set up an Educational Council to inquire into and plan a possible system of alternative education. And the ANC is continuing the state of boycott. Five teachers were arrested in Germiston location after allegedly conducting an 'illegal school' attended by 'banned' pupils. Government syllabuses have not yet come into operation. And yet so much has happened. How much more when schools teach 'Bantu Education' proper? □

Photograph by Bob Gosani

An open-air class at the Haile Selassie School in Alexandra, which has been a private school for the last five years.

Verwoerd spelt out the meaning of the Bantu Education Act in 1953. 'There is no place for the Bantu in the European community above the level of certain forms of labour . . . it is of no avail for him to receive a training which draws him away from his own community and misleads him by showing him the green pastures of the Europeans but still does not allow him to graze there . . . This leads to the much-discussed frustration of educated natives who can find no employment which is acceptable to them . . . it must be replaced by planned Bantu education . . . with its roots entirely in the native areas and in the native environment and community.'

The girl who will not go to school again

Drum: April 1955 For 12-year-old Elizabeth Ngwendu, of Edith Street, Sophiatown, there will be no more school after the Easter holidays. From 1 April, all African education will be transferred to the Bantu Education Department. And Elizabeth's father, Mr Bob Ngwendu, a member of the Transvaal Executive of the ANC, has decided that she will stay at home until Africans once more get a full education, even if that is many years in the future. In the meantime, after 1 April, Elizabeth will receive 'illicit education' from her parents in their home.

Until now Elizabeth has been in standard five at St Cyprians School, one of the Anglican schools that will be closed down as a result of the Bantu Education Act. She could have changed to a government school and later gone to high school, as her parents had originally planned for her. Later, perhaps, there was Fort Hare . . . and a profession. But now her career must stop.

Drum interviewed Mr Ngwendu – 'Old Bob' as his colleagues call him – a relentless, hardworking Congress organiser. This is what he had to say: 'As a loyal Congressite I abide by the Durban resolution of our national movement which condemns Bantu Education and calls on all Africans to boycott schools. I won't send my child to school because I don't want her to be subjected to an educational system that must eventually corrupt her mind. I don't want my daughter to think herself any different from children of other African races as a result of the ethnic groupings on which Bantu Education is based; I don't want her to feel inferior to any European child – which this kind of education is meant to stamp on every African's mind. I want her to be taught the things that all other decent self-respecting human beings in the rest of the world would

For Elizabeth Ngwendu, the 'Congress Girl', there will be no more learning at a classroom desk after 1 April, when the Bantu Education Act takes effect.

Rather no education at all than Bantu Education, says Congress father

like to learn, the things that enrich the mind and deepen character, so that she should know and appreciate that she belongs to the whole human race. For these reasons, I am withdrawing my daughter from school to show my strong disapproval of Bantu Education, and my wife and I will teach her at home. I could send her to some other school here or in the country, but I stand on principle.'

Mr Ngwendu himself organised delegates from Sophiatown to attend last month's 'Save our children' conference, held at the Orlando Communal Hall. The theme of the conference was 'We want universal not Bantu Education'. Delegates were to decide what to do in the light of the Congress resolution taken in Durban to boycott schools, followed by the ANC National Executive's subsequent decision to postpone the boycott. The meeting decided that the boycott strategy should be pursued. Mr Ngwendu and P Q Vundla were among prominent people who promised to withdraw their children from school.

This was one of several meetings being held all over the country by parents on the same issue. Parents are becoming more and more interested in what their children are taught in schools, something that could not have happened five years ago.

The government, on the other hand, is determined to go through with the system and to make it work. It maintains that 'Bantu Education' was planned to help the child to adapt himself to the society in which he lives and suppress whatever hopes he may have of being the equal of the white man. This, the government says, will save the child from frustration, because in the present set-up, he cannot be allowed to do jobs that are specially for Europeans and cannot live among white people. □

Transvaal ANC Executive member Bob Ngwendu has decided that his child will not go to a 'say-baas-to-the-white-man' kind of school.

26 June 1955

The people's delegates meet in Kliptown

Three thousand delegates arrived at the Congress of the People from all over the country. Here, the Alexandra delegation arrives.

Drum: August 1955 The rumblings of the Congress of the People are over. Some people feel that 26 June was an immense success. Others feel that there was a good deal of emotional talk. Whatever the case may be, it was clear that there was a marked spirit of get-togetherness at Kliptown and a desire for an outlet among the 3 000 delegates.

The idea of drawing up a Freedom Charter was originally that of Professor Z K Matthews. At the Cape Provincial Congress in August 1953, he suggested the summoning of a 'national convention at which all the groups might be represented to consider our national problems on an all-inclusive basis' to 'draw up a Freedom Charter for the democratic South Africa of the future'. The ANC's annual conference in Queenstown later that year agreed to implement his idea. A few months later the Executives of the African Congress, the Indian Congress, the Congress of Democrats (white) and the new South African Coloured People's Organisation met and decided to establish a National Action Council for the Congress of the People, made up of eight delegates from each of the sponsoring organisations. Chief Luthuli told *Drum* in an exclusive interview: 'The Congress of the People is entirely a Congress idea, to which others are invited in accordance with our principles.'

The council went about organising the collection of popular demands from people all over the country and then the council sorted out the demands which were drawn up into a Charter by a drafting committee.

The Congress of the people draft the Freedom Charter

Photographs by Peter Magubane and Bob Gosani

The delegation from the Western Areas.

On 26 June 1955, 3 000 delegates from all over the country gathered near the coloured township of Kliptown to discuss the Charter. The Kliptown football ground was a field of bright black, green and yellow colours in flags and uniform ties. Congress 'freedom' songs were sung at every pause in the proceedings. Many speakers on the Freedom Charter on 26 June, noted that the day might not be far off when its demands would be met; the road might be long, but a united democratic front was the only solution. ANC President Albert Luthuli, in his message read to the Congress, said among other things that 'it should have been plain to the architects of the Union that by excluding from the orbit of democracy, the majority of the population, the non-whites, they were laying a false foundation for the new state and making a mockery of democracy to call such a state democratic'.

When the armed police arrived and came forward to the grandstand to conduct a search, a leading speaker was introducing the item of the Charter that says 'There shall be peace and friendship.' The police took down the names and addresses of everyone present and confiscated many documents.

The delegates to the Congress of the People have been instructed to take the Freedom Charter to their people, explain it to them, encourage them to know it by heart so that it becomes a guide.

Among the countries that sent messages of goodwill were the Sudan, India and China. Persons and organisa-

The watchers: Thousands sat in the sun to witness the full proceedings of the Congress of the People at Kliptown, Johannesburg.

tions in America, Britain, Belgium and France also sent messages.

Several people are asking what the future of the Congress of the People is. Has it definitely come to an end with the drawing up of the Freedom Charter? Or has it come to stay? Why four distinct organisations? And so on. Well, some behind-the-scenes movement has been going on about this very point. There has been much confidential talk in certain circles among the four member bodies that they should eventually become one big organisation. The present bodies would fall away. They regard that as the only logical result. A number of officials in the four organisations feel, however, that they want to tread slowly because there are conservative sections of political opinion among the Africans, Indians, coloureds and Europeans. □

Ezekiel Mphahlele

'. . . South Africa belongs to all who live in it, black and white! . . . And we pledge ourselves to strive together, sparing neither strength nor courage, until the democratic changes set out here have been won'

Photographs by Peter Magubane and Bob Gosani

ANC Natal leader Dr Conco, one of Chief Luthuli's aides. The Chief and Dr Dadoo, President of the SAIC, could not attend because both were banned.

Peter Beyleveld, President of the Congress of Democrats (SACOD). Beyleveld later became a state witness against Braam Fischer, and against Congress at other trials.

The Charter

The Freedom Charter, which the Congress of the People had met to present, was adopted by the four organisations. It says that:

The people shall govern;
All national groups shall have equal rights;
The people shall share in the country's wealth;
The land shall be shared among those who work it;
All shall be equal before the law;
All shall enjoy equal human rights;
There shall be work and security;
The doors of learning and culture shall be opened;
There shall be houses, security and comfort;
There shall be peace and friendship.

Ronald Press, member of the Congress of Democrats. The SACOD identified itself more strongly with the Soviet Bloc than did the other members of the Congress Alliance.

Almost 7 000 children were expelled from school because of their protest against the Bantu Education Act

Drum: November 1955 The ANC has been vacillating regarding its strategy for opposing Bantu Education. Its annual conference in 1954 called on African parents to prepare to 'withdraw their children from primary schools indefinitely as from 1 April 1955 until a further directive from the National Executive Committee (NEC)'. A bit later, however, the NEC decided that there was no evidence that the country would be ready for withdrawal on 1 April.

However, there was popular support for a boycott in some areas and so the NEC met again and accepted that parents could withdraw their children from school in areas where people were prepared and where alternative activities for children had been arranged. The scattered boycott, which is still continuing, began on 12 April. Some boycotts have been prolonged, and others have begun and ended sporadically. About 7 000 children have been expelled from school and more than 100 teachers have lost their jobs.

There has been an enthusiastic response in Benoni, Germiston, Brakpan, Alexandra, Moroka and Natalspruit (Transvaal) and some active protest in Bethlehem (OFS) and the Port Elizabeth area. Local ANC organisers and volunteers have set up a few alternative 'cultural clubs' for expelled and boycotting pupils but the police have been raiding these and harassing the club 'leaders'.

People from various political organisations, educationists, church denominations, private individuals, have joined to form the National Education Movement. The function of this movement is to draw up 'lectures' and programmes of activities aimed at giving the rebel children a wide range of general knowledge. □

Throughout the country protest meetings are held. 'We don't want passes!' the women are shouting

'How can the issue of reference books to African women be an oppressive measure?' asked a statement by the Native Affairs Department in 1955, when the campaign against passes for women was at its height. Perhaps an answer can be supplied by the women of the Cape.

It was just before six in the morning when Mrs Alice Qwela heard the police hammering on the door of her shanty in Nyanga demanding to see passes. As one policeman was about to burst into the room, Mrs Qwela tried to hold the door closed. 'Just wait while I put some clothes on,' she said. Mrs Qwela was six months pregnant. But the policeman, an African, would not wait. He punched Mrs Qwela in the eye, knocking her down, and went in. Mrs Qwela's pass was in order, and she was allowed to go – to the doctor to have her injuries treated.

Many women whose passes are not in order end up in prison. The cells themselves are cold in winter, and without furniture. And although each police station has a matron officially appointed to it, none of the women had ever met her during the time they were detained. They were solely in the hands of male policemen.

The very business of getting a pass has been made into a punishment and an ordeal. They wait and wait. For hours and hours. Sometimes for a whole day. Most of them have babies and children with them. As the sun gets higher, the cries and quarrelling get louder. And when you do get in, it is often a tired, impatient – sometimes abusive – official who deals with you. 'You have enough children now, Annie. You must stop sleeping with your husband.' Sometimes, the hundreds of women sitting just outside the yard of these offices become impatient. They form a crowd and start singing *'Nkosi Sikelele Afrika.* □

Throughout 1955 there were protests against the whole spectrum of unjust laws – protests against forced removals, against passes, against the Group Areas Act, against Bantu Education and against poverty

In August 1955, after months of campaigning on the issue of passes, the Transvaal branch of the Federation of South African Women decided to mount a demonstration in Pretoria against unjust laws

On the platform, Rahima Moosa (sitting left), Josie Palmer and Helen Joseph (dark glasses).

September 1955

Police raids on the Congress

The police raiding the offices of the South African Indian Congress. The countrywide police raids of 27 September 1955 followed closely on the Congress of the People meeting in Kliptown. The police confiscated thousands of documents during their searches. On the wall of the office is a photograph of Dr Ganghathura 'Monty' Naicker, leader of the Indian Congress, and a picture, flanked by red flags, of Mao Tse Tung.

Barney Desai during an Indian Congress meeting: 'In the absence of parliamentary means of getting redress for our problems, we must demonstrate. It is time government is shown we oppose "whites only" rule.' Ahmed Kathrada (seated) and Nelson Mandela.

Nelson Mandela during the campaign against passes for women: 'When the men are fired, when the men are sent to jail, the women can still care for the children. But what of the babies when the women must themselves go to prison?'

'We are anticipating a period when the Congress will be forced to operate as a clandestine movement,' said Nelson Mandela in late 1955. Youth leader Peter Nthite (left).

The Evaton People's Transport Council, headed by Vus Umzi Make as Chairman (right) and Joe Molefi as Secretary (left), came into being to organise and steer the bus boycott movement in Evaton.

Jordan Ngubane of the ANC reveals some of the differences between Congressmen

Drum: December 1955 Congressmen are not of one mind as to the form of the next phase of the struggle against racial oppression. Very many of them realise frankly that if the differences which divide them at the moment cannot be solved soon, the Congress will become a thing of the past. If, on the other hand, the Luthuli regime could bring to bear on the situation that breadth of vision and genius for statesmanship it showed during the early stages of the Resistance Campaign, the Congress could emerge stronger than it has ever been in the past.

Why have these differences developed at this particular time in the history of the Congress? In my view, it is because the Resistance Campaign produced results for which neither the Congress nor the masses had prepared themselves. Let us take only one such consequence of the Campaign: the new responsibilities it laid on the shoulders of the ANC. The response of about 8 500 men and women to Dr Moroka's call for volunteers in the Defiance Campaign exceeded the expectations not only of Congress leaders but also of very many people on all sides of the colour line. This show of African strength altered the balance of political power in this country. Almost overnight the initiative to set the pace of political progress slipped into African hands.

White liberals and progressives saw in the response of the masses to Dr Moroka's call the advent of the great moment. For them, non-violence had created an atmosphere where the white democrat could cross the colour line to join hands with the black democrat in the fight against *Herrenvolkism*. That is the background to the emergence of the Liberal Party and later, the Congress of Democrats. This transformed the fight against *Herrenvolkism* into the fight of all just men against injustice; it ceased to be merely the African people's struggle against tyranny of race. This was a setback for those who insisted on seeing the struggle from the perspective of rigid African nationalism. Since the coloured, the Indian and the European had proved themselves reliable fighters for democracy by the side of the African, the Congress could not reject their outstretched hand of friendship without becoming racialistic. If the Congress became racialistic, what point was there in opposing apartheid?

The Congress did the right thing morally and politically. It accepted the hand of friendship and in that way gave substance and form to the ideal of partnership. This was a positive gesture of African goodwill and an act of good faith. The question which remained unanswered in all this, however, was: On what ideological basis was partnership to be founded? Here Congressmen differed very sharply. Most of the ANC's present internal difficulties centre around this question.

Four different forces are at work competing for the acceptance of their respective ideologies as the basis of partnership. The Leftists have staked a very strong claim for a Marxist basis. So much so that there was introduced into the Freedom Charter the principle of nationalisation – something which commits the ANC as one of the sponsors of the Congress of the People to a new principle of economic policy. From the Centre have come the liberals. For them partnership can be established only on a liberal democratic basis. Then there are those who teach that the people of Africa belong together and as such should stand together against white domination on the African continent. Their goal is 'Africa for the Africans'. A fourth force is composed of those who see in the ideal of a common destiny for the man of colour in the world the only hope for the African. As a result they work for closer bonds between the peoples of Asia and those of Africa. Whatever the outcome of the present struggle for dominance inside the Congress, the old type of Congress has gone never to return. From this point African nationalism can either become racialistic in the way that Afrikaner nationalism is, or embrace the ideal of equal partnership in ways which will be more reassuring to the racial minorities.

In the meantime, much depends on the outcome of the quarrel between the Centre and the Left in Congress over the Freedom Charter. The Left insists that adoption of the Charter at Kliptown bound the sponsoring bodies to accept the Charter as their own and straightaway presses for its being signed by a million people. These tactics are designed to confront the ANC's Centre wing with the accomplished fact of nationalisation having been accepted and the Charter signed by a million people – most of them Congressmen. The Centre takes the view that adoption of the Charter at Kliptown was merely acknowledgement of its existence. To be binding on the sponsoring bodies, their national conferences had to ratify it, after which it could be signed.

The real significance of the tactics of the Left lies in their calculation to place Mr Luthuli (a known Centre man) and his personal followers in an extremely awkward position. It remains to be seen what he will do if the National Conference of the ANC, which meets in December, decides that the nationalisation of industry, the mines and the banks – as demanded in the Freedom Charter – is the new Congress line. □

Photograph by Jurgen Schadeberg

Jordan K Ngubane, well-known writer and ANC leader, tells what's really going on behind the peaceful-looking Congress scene. Ngubane, a founder of the ANC Youth League, later became an outspoken critic of the ANC and joined the Liberal Party because he believed that the ANC was becoming too prone to communist influence.

95

December 1955

The ANC holds its Annual Conference in Bloemfontein

Drum: February 1956 What a buzzing number of topics brought the works to a standstill at the ANC conference at Bloemfontein in December last year! The conference kept on so long talking about other things that it could never really get down to dynamic issues and – more important – setting down a line of action.

Messages of goodwill from friendly organisations took hours to read and to interpret into African languages. Like a woman's petticoat, domestic quarrels of certain branches kept jutting out, like the difficult Alexandra branch. The question of who was the official delegation and who wasn't kept up a nagging tune. The *Bantu World* was shown the door, but not before a good bit of wrangling.

The Rev J Calata, who presided, lost control. Several items jumped out of their rightful places on the agenda and came up for discussion before their time. The only thing there didn't seem time for was action.

Still, for all its lack of direction and inefficiency, the Congress is still the vital rallying point for thousands of Africans who think seriously about politics. Even critics of the Congress are prepared to stay there. Many well-known Congress leaders were absent because of their bans and mention of their names continually evoked the cry, 'Mayibuye!' Chief Albert Luthuli was actually re-elected President by an unanimous vote, although he was absent. This, in spite of a rumour that the Transvaal had 'built up' somebody else for presidency.

What were the main things that Congress did use its time on?

The Xuma letter

First, there was 'that letter' from Dr A B Xuma, ANC President until 1949. The letter of 'good wishes' that caused so much hullaballoo. The letter that wished the conference success and also took the opportunity to give the Congress a scrubbing. A number of delegates, including the 'Africanists', realised that the Executive did not intend to read the letter. The Executive knew what the letter contained. So did the Africanists. 'We want the letter read!' they said. The argument dragged on deep into the night. Finally the Executive decided to read only extracts

Mr Robert Resha, national leader of the Youth League, who clashed with Africanist, Dr Peter Tsele, at the conference.

Photographs by Peter Magubane

Dr Moroka, no longer on the conference platform, addressing the Congress as an ordinary delegate.

Dr Peter Tsele, one of those who led the Africanists at the conference: 'Congress must go back to its 1949 Programme of Action'.

The women at the conference were dressed in costumes and robes that blended the Congress colours of black, green and yellow.

Professor Z K Matthews, National Executive member, supported the 'Africanist' contingent in calling for a boycott of advisory and school boards.

Woolly resolutions, acrimonious exchanges and little action

from the letter. Dr Xuma accused the ANC of losing its distinct African identity and criticised its alliance with the congresses of other races. 'One hears or reads of statements by the "Congresses" and one hardly ever gets the standpoint of the ANC,' he said.

Can the Congress stand up to criticism? 'The ANC,' says the doctor, 'seems to fear facing criticism – constructive and otherwise – from its following and others. People are referred to as "sellers-out" or "agents" or "friends of the government" instead of being shown where they are wrong.' Furthermore, Dr Xuma said, 'The Congress leadership seems to have turned their backs on the nation-building programme of the 1940s.'

And the Congress's strategy?

'By acting on principles of action for action's sake and for propaganda reasons instead of aiming at achieving results, Congress, through the Defiance Campaign, the Western Areas Removal Scheme and the school boycott, aroused vain hopes and made promises of secret weapons. If leaders arouse the masses, and the leaders then fail the masses in the testing hour, the loyalty and faith of the masses is shaken.' He then appealed to the conference to drop its resolution to boycott schools.

Africanists versus Freedom Charterists

The old story of Africanism versus the Congress of the People came up again. The Africa-for-Africans group (Africanists) discharged its buckshot saying: 'Congress must go back to its 1949 Programme of Action'.

Dr Peter Tsele and Messrs R Sobukwe, J Molefi and P Lebalo led the Africanists. According to them, the idea of the Congress of the People and the Freedom Charter is an illustration that the ANC is no longer 'Africanist' and has allowed 'foreign ideologies' to direct its affairs. It was for this reason that they found they were on a common platform with Dr Xuma and pressed that his letter should be read.

The Africanists have sprung from the now almost defunct Youth League. After the Youth League had got rid of the Old Guard, which included Dr Xuma, and took over the leadership of the ANC, the League seemed to find no further reason to live an active life. It almost completely stopped criticising the Congress.

The Africanists have suddenly revived the late Lembede's nationalism. They are against such close co-operation with Indians, coloureds and Europeans as may give these minorities a share in dictating Congress policy.

The battle raged. The Africanists proposed a resolution calling upon all members of advisory boards, school boards, *bungas* and other State institutions set up for Africans only, to resign from these bodies. If they did not, they should be expelled. This was based on one of the provisions of the 1949 Programme of Action. The ANC has always put off this item of the Programme.

Significantly, Professor Matthews, a member of the National Executive, and Rev W S Gawe, Queenstown President of the Cape Provincial ANC, supported the 'Africanist' group on the resolution to boycott advisory and school boards. They lost the day when the resolution was put off to the next annual conference in December 1956. Some advisory board men argued that if they resigned, 'stooges' would take their place. Other delegates argued that there were too few delegates left to resolve such a big issue. Some of the Africanists were actually delegates to the conference, and they mean to stay on and criticise the Congress from within.

Woolly resolutions

A number of big issues were either glossed over or deferred to future conferences. There were a number of woolly resolutions which did not commit the ANC to any programme of action. One resolution gave out a vague order to branches to withdraw children from school 'when they are ready to boycott Bantu Education'.

The adoption of the Freedom Charter was also postponed, although the ANC succeeded in starting things moving towards a point where it will be embarrassing to reject the Charter. The collection of a million signatures for the Charter is to go on. Discussion has to go on at a provincial level, and the ANC resolved to form a permanent co-ordinating committee to bring about closer co-operation among the partners of the Congress of the People. The only thing that may put a break to the movement towards a united front of coloureds, Africans, Indians and Europeans will be the stand of the Africanists. It is most likely that if they become a force at all, their Africa-for-Africans doctrine will draw support from young intellectuals.

The women brought gay new fashion to the ANC Congress – and also bright new political ideas!

Fashion leaders, the Executive of the ANC Women's League are: Mrs Lilian Ngoyi (President), Mrs M Molefi (Durban), Miss F Mkhize (Durban), Mrs V Gqirana (Port Elizabeth), Mrs C A N Kuse (Queenstown), and Mrs Frances Baard (Port Elizabeth).

The women were at the conference in grand style. They wore garments that blended the Congress colours of black, green and yellow in all conceivable patterns and styles of skirt, frock, blouse and headgear. There were lots of variations of this colour theme on long flowing skirts and shawls and stoles, which have become an African tradition. This showed that the women are setting the standard of fashion in Congress uniforms.

On the political plane, too, women have come to the fore. They are making their voice heard in the affairs of the ANC. For the laws of the country have now started pots and pans rattling in the kitchen, and a number of things are on the boil. Passes for women, for instance, and the schooling of their children under Bantu Education, are worrying their minds.

'Leave us to handle this as women,' said some. 'We will not carry passes,' said others, and 'Our daily life is bitter enough, we don't find rest.' 'Our men are humiliated enough: what should we do when the time comes for us to carry passes?', others asked. There will be a special conference early this year to discuss 'Passes for women'. Each provincial branch of the ANC Women's League has to organise an anti-pass campaign. A national council of action will also be formed to co-ordinate the activities of all Congress in an anti-pass campaign. □

Ezekiel Mphahlele

Lilian Ngoyi – The most talked-of woman in politics

Drum: March 1956 'She's ambitious!' 'She's a remarkable orator!' 'She knows too little about political theory!' 'She has a brilliant intellect!' 'What kind of woman is this?' 'She almost rocks men out of their pants when she speaks!' So say people about Mrs Lilian Ngoyi, now President of the ANC Women's League for the second term – the most talked-of woman in politics.

Who is Lilian Ngoyi? The woman factory worker who is tough granite on the outside, but soft and compassionate deep down in her. The woman who three years ago was hardly known in non-European politics. The woman whose rise to fame has been phenomenal.

Born in 1911 in Pretoria of Bapedi parents, Mrs Ngoyi grew up in conditions of abject poverty. Her father, now dead, changed employment and the Matabane family moved to a mine in the Eastern Transvaal. Her mother, still alive today, did washing for whites. Little Lilian was noted to be the biggest crier in the neighbourhood. She would cry until she fainted.

She was sent to Kilnerton Training Institution while she was still in Standard Two. She reached the first year of the teachers' course but her father couldn't afford the fees any longer, and so she had to quit school. Lilian then went to City Deep mine hospital to train as a nurse. She later got married, but after a few years her husband, Mr Ngoyi, died.

Except for a short interlude of ballroom dancing in the competition ranks, her life slid into a quiet slow tempo. But a hectic political career began in 1952, when the ANC launched its Defiance Campaign. Mrs Ngoyi left a critically sick daughter in hospital to join a batch that went to 'defy' apartheid regulations at the General Post Office. She told inquiring officials and the police that she was writing a telegram to some cabinet ministers. The defiers were acquitted and Mrs Ngoyi then began to organise Orlando women for Congress.

As Vice-President of the South African Federation of Women, Mrs Ngoyi was the chosen delegate to the Lausanne conference of women in Switzerland last year. Together with another African woman, she visited several European countries on both sides of the Iron Curtain.

Mrs Ngoyi is the first African woman to be on the Transvaal Provincial Executive of the ANC and on the National Executive.

In 1954 she became Treasurer of the South African Non-European Council of Trade Unions. She is a member of the Women's Garment Workers' Union for the Reef, and

Lilian Ngoyi, who has the stubbornness of a centipede that climbs in the same direction despite any attempts to alter its course.

'My womb is shaken when they speak of Bantu Education!'

is also currently Acting President of the SA Federation of Women.

Once in politics, Mrs Ngoyi knew that the nameless compulsion that had been working in her since childhood had become a reality. Those days she loved to read about pioneers who led their people to freedom. Not least, she was thrilled by the activities of Hebrew leaders in the Bible. Another thing that made a lasting impact on her was the migrant labour system as she saw men come and go between the reserves and the mines.

Her father was bitterly anti-white. Strong passion expresses itself through her too, but in the more meaningful form of anti-oppression – whether practised by whites or non-whites.

Mrs Ngoyi's weakness lies in being highly emotional. Her strength lies in the fact that she admits it and is always prepared to be disciplined and to submit to cold logic. She also admits her weak educational background. She is therefore not much of a political thinker, but she gets down to a job in a manner that shames many a political theorist. For this woman has bundles and bundles of energy. Granite reinforced with wire. She will often begin her family washing at ten in the night – home cleanliness and sewing are a religious passion with her.

Mrs Ngoyi is a brilliant orator. She can toss an audience on her little finger, get men grunting with shame and a feeling of smallness, and infuse everyone with renewed courage. Her speech always teems with vivid figures of speech. Mrs Ngoyi will say: 'We don't want men who wear skirts under their trousers. If they don't want to act, let us women exchange garments with them.' Or she will say: 'We women are like hens that lay eggs for somebody to take away. That's the effect of Bantu Education.'

At a recent anti-pass meeting one masculine firebrand advocated violence as a political solution. Mrs Ngoyi replied: 'Shed your own blood first and let's see what stuff it's made of.' She denounced violence as stupid and impractical. The firebrand spluttered, flickered and sat down to smoulder, feeling embarrassed.

Guts and granite are required to lead and inspire the thousands of women who are everywhere resisting the extension of the pass system to women. The heat and pressure of the times have provided a Lilian Ngoyi to perform that function. □

Ezekiel Mphahlele

Lilian Ngoyi and her grandchild Memory. She has led and inspired thousands of women who have now come to the front line of African politics.

Women demonstrate against passes

'We have not come here to beg or plead, but to ask for what is our right as mothers, as women and as citizens of our country'

Drum: September 1956 Last year, on 27 October 1955, two thousand women demonstrated against the pass laws at the Union Buildings in Pretoria. They carried letters of protest to the Office of the Minister of Native Affairs. Almost a year later, on 9 August 1956, 20 000 women of all races, from the cities and towns, from reserves and villages, took a petition addressed to the Prime Minister to the Union Buildings in Pretoria. He was not in. Their petition demanded of Strijdom that the pass laws be abolished. It was the most spectacular demonstration that the women have staged since it became clear a couple of years ago that the government was to impose reference books on them. Up to then they had been far less restricted than their men-folk in their movement.

Many of the women carried babies on their backs. The majority were from the Transvaal, but at least 200 had come from other provinces, including Chief Luthuli's wife with a group from Stanger, Natal. Helen Joseph, Lilian Ngoyi, Rahima Moosa and Sophie Williams left the petitions outside the empty office of the Minister of Native Affairs. The women waited in the forecourt of the Union Buildings in silence for half an hour, and then sang together 'Strijdom, you have tampered with the women, you have struck a rock!' Civil servants, milling about and witnessing the scene, looked astonished. Then the women quietly left.

Some of the 2 000 women walking up to the Union Buildings in Pretoria on 27 October 1955 to tell the government what they thought of its plans to make them carry passes.

Luthuli: 'When the women begin to take an active part in the struggle, as they are doing now, no power on earth can stop us from achieving freedom in our lifetime'

Photographs by Jurgen Schadeberg

'We, the women of South Africa, have come here today . . . We are women from every part of South Africa. We are women of every race, we come from the cities and the towns, from the reserves and the villages. We come as women united in our purpose to save the African woman from the degradation of passes.'

The text of the petition the women delivered on 9 August 1956

We, the women of South Africa, have come here today. We represent and we speak on behalf of hundreds of thousands of women who could not be with us. But all over the country, at this moment, women are watching and thinking of us. Their hearts are with us.

We are women from every part of South Africa. We are women of every race, we come from the cities and the towns, from the reserves and the villages. We come as women united in our purpose to save the African woman from the degradation of passes. For hundreds of years the African people have suffered under the most bitter law of all – the pass law – which has brought untold suffering to every African family.

Raids, arrests, loss of pay, long hours at the pass office, weeks in the cells awaiting trial, forced farm labour – this is what the pass laws have brought to African men. Punishment and misery – not for a crime, but for the lack of a pass. We African women know too well the effect of this law upon our homes, our children. We, who are not African women, know how our sisters suffer.

Your government proclaims aloud at home and abroad that the pass laws have been abolished, but we women know this is not true, for our husbands, our brothers, our sons are still being arrested, thousands every day, under these very pass laws. It is only the name that has changed. The "reference book" and the pass are one. In March 1952 your Minister of Native Affairs denied in Parliament that a law would be introduced which would force African women to carry passes. But in 1956 your government is attempting to force passes upon the African women, and we are here today to protest against this insult to all women. For to us an insult to African women is an insult to all women.

We want to tell you what the pass would mean to an African woman, and we want you to know that whether you call it a reference book, an identity book, or by any other disguising name, to us it is a *Pass*. And it means just this:

- That homes will be broken up when women are arrested under pass laws.
- That children will be left uncared for, helpless, and mothers will be torn from their babies for failure to produce a pass.
- That women and young girls will be exposed to humiliation and degradation at the hands of pass-searching policemen.
- That women will lose their right to move freely from one place to another.

In the name of women of South Africa, we say to you, each one of us, African, European, Indian and coloured, that we are opposed to the pass system. We, voters and voteless, call upon your government not to issue passes to African women. We shall not rest until *all* pass laws and all forms of permits restricting our freedom have been abolished. We shall not rest until we have won for our children their fundamental rights of freedom, justice and security.

The organisations spearheading this protest are the Federation of South African Women, formed in April 1954, and the ANC Women's League. They have been organising women everywhere to resist passes. Less than a year ago, in October 1955, there was a similar march to the Union Buildings of 2 000 Transvaal women who left petitions for the Minister of Native Affairs. Since the government's mobile units started issuing women with reference books, there have been spirited demonstrations by women throughout the country. Earlier this year, at Winburg in the Orange Free State, women who said they had been tricked into taking out passes went to the offices of the location superintendent and burnt their passes. In numerous places women have marched from the locations to the offices of town clerks, Native Commissioners, magistrates and location superintendents to hand in petitions of protest. □

'To us, an insult to African women is an insult to all women'

Photographs by Jurgen Schadeberg

On 27 October 1955, watched by 2 000 protesters and some bewildered State employees, the four representatives, Rahima Moosa, Lilian Ngoyi, Helen Joseph and Sophie Williams – one from each race group – walked up to the government offices . . . and left the petitions outside the office of the Minister of Native Affairs.

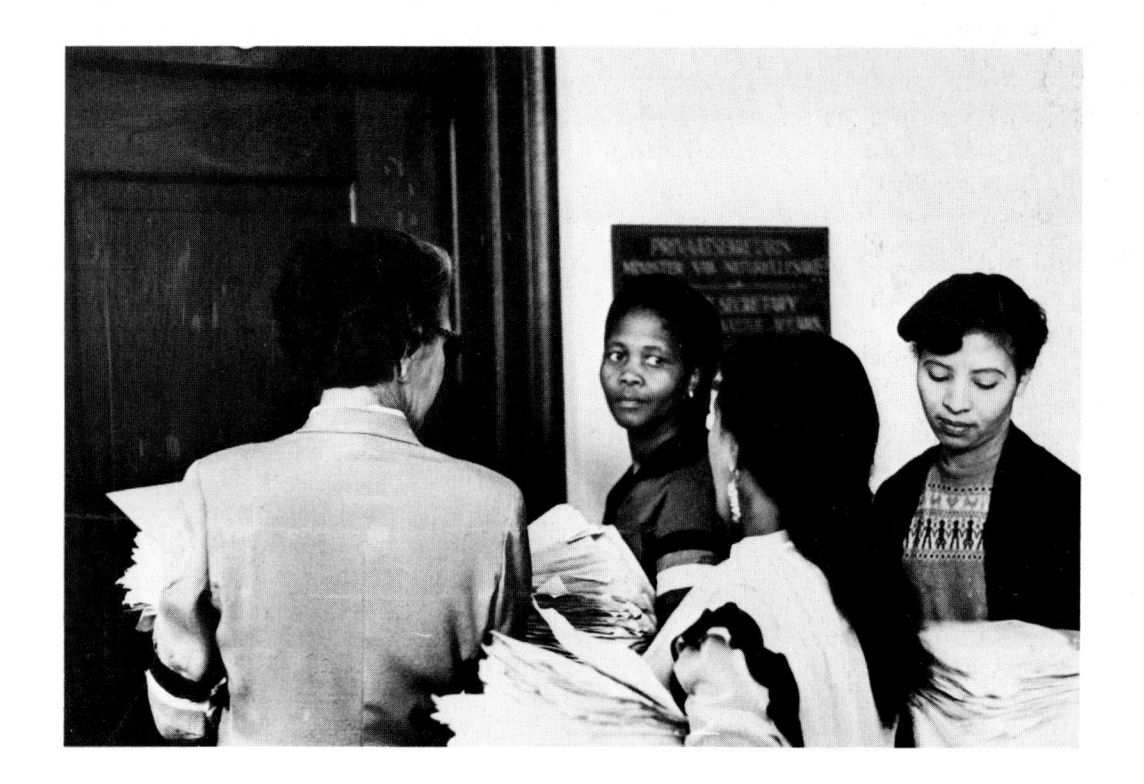

105

Countrywide arrests for treason

'You are under arrest!' Sampie Molope was arrested by Major Spengler at the Sophiatown meeting of the People's Defence Committee.

Ida Mutwana, ANC songleader. The preparatory trial opened in the Drill Hall in Johannesburg two weeks after the arrests. There were huge demonstrations outside the Court.

Natal ANC leader Dorothy Nyembe and S Damons, SAPCO member. Each time a police van stopped and expelled a batch of accused, the crowd gave them a thunderous welcome.

Cape leader Frances Baard. The hearing began with the 156 accused locked in a cage. Someone put a placard 'Don't Feed' on the cage.

Can Themba asks what strange forms Congress action will take now

Photographs by Alf Kumalo, Peter Magubane, Gopal Naransamy and Jurgen Schadeberg

Who will lead the congresses now?

Drum: January 1957 At dawn on Wednesday, 5 December 1956, the South African police, equipped with warrants signed by a Johannesburg magistrate, swooped down on several political leaders and arrested them on a charge of high treason. Many political organisations were caught off-balance. So *Drum* rushed out to find out what they were going to do. This is a report by Can Themba on what moves several organisations have been considering.

The police operation was spectacular! In one of the fastest moves, one of the greatest political raids this country has ever known, the political personalities were rounded up by the Special Branch of the CID and charged in the Johannesburg Magistrate's Court with high treason – the most serious offence in any country.

And that one dramatic act has hurled up three wet-net words in the political language of the Union – 'black-banding', 'rabbitting' and 'The Ghost Committee' – words that may have a tremendous significance for South Africa.

The suggestion has already been made that people should wear on their left arms black bands of mourning. It is not known as yet whether the functioning executives will accept and proclaim this suggestion. Since the active executives of the Congresses may now be out of action, hushed whispers of going underground have been made on the Reef. It is felt by supporters that only by burrowing underground like rabbits can the Congresses win a breather to consider their next moves. This would bring a new phase to the political tactics of the Congresses.

Outside the Drill Hall, on the opening day of the trial there were violent scenes as police and spectators provoked each other, causing the Court to adjourn.

Always they have declared that their policies and methods are above-board and that they have nothing to hide. But now they might decide to walk by night and act in the dark. There are still serious doubts as to whether the organisations have not been so finally beheaded by the raids that they will not be able to find the personnel for future leadership. There is also the fear that if the most responsible leaders are put out of action, 'won't more reckless characters take over?'

Hours after the raids on that sultry morning of Wednesday, 5 December, rumours were already rife that certain organisations were considering setting up 'ghost committees', that is, committees that would not be announced to the world, but would take up the task of organising the Congresses, keeping them intact, sending out information and directives.

As far as the rest of the country is concerned, the people are stunned. Some people have taken the point of view that the Congresses are dead. Others have argued that Congresses that were already declining because of their ineffectiveness have become famous and real. They say that now they know their Congresses are representative bodies of the people. But in the first few days of the raids, the people were thoroughly shaken.

At the first burst of dawn, the police raided the homes of over 100 people. They searched their houses, removed documents, books, magazines and, in many cases, their owners. One of the most startling arrests was that of a

The beginning of a treason trial that was to last more than four years

Photographs by Alf Kumalo, Peter Magubane, Gopal Naransamy and Jurgen Schadeberg

At the Fort prison, Johannesburg's forbidding gaol high on a hill.

Member of Parliament, Mr L B Lee-Warden (Natives Representative, Cape Western). But then there were Chief A J Luthuli, the Rev D C Thompson, Professor Z K Matthews and son Joe. By the end of the first day about 150 people had been arrested. This was it!

When the accused came before the magistrate, spectators packed the public seats in steaming heat. Just before the proceedings started there was a brisk hum of chatter, but one felt behind it all the tense atmosphere, the pent-up feelings of relatives and friends and the curious, and perhaps those who feared for themselves in the future. The accused came up in batches of twenty, some of them cheerful, some sullen, some frightened, some bewildered, some consumed in high wrath. When Nelson Mandela, attorney at law, came up, he hunched his shoulders and seemed to glower with suppressed anger. They were all formally charged with high treason and remanded to 19 December 1956.

Other people arrested in various parts of the country were being sent to Johannesburg, afterwards being remanded there to appear in a preparatory examination. All have been remanded in custody at the Fort, Johannesburg's Central Prison. Everybody regards this as the most dramatic single piece of police action in the Union. And everybody is watching the case with keyed interest. □

Can Themba

DRUM: FEBRUARY 195[?]

ANC: African National Congress. CP: Cape. COD: Congress of Democrats. M.P.: Member of Parliament. M.P.C.: Member of Provincial Council. NIC: Natal.

TVL

- J. Slovo, advocate.
- R. First (Mrs. Slovo).
- Frank Madiba, banned man.
- P. P. D. Nokwe, advocate.
- P. J. Hodgson, C.O.D. member.
- Jonas Matlou, A.N.C. member.
- Helen Joseph, women's leader.
- Patrick Molao[?], Youth League[?]
- Robert Resha, journalist.
- Oliver Tambo, lawyer.
- J. Poo, A.N.C. member.
- Suliman Esakjee, T.I.C. member.
- William Ngwendu, A.N.C. member.
- Fish Keitsing, A.N.C. member.
- A. E. Patel, T.I.C. member.
- Andrew Chamile, A.N.C. member.
- Mary Ranta, women's leader.
- Bernard Seitsh[?], A.N.C. member
- Piet Mokgofe, anti-religious.
- Marks Shope, A.N.C. member.
- J. Makwe, A.N.C. member.
- M. Mpho, A.N.C. member.
- Moosa Moolla, slogan-writer.
- H. Tshabalala, Youth Leaguer.
- Jerry Kumalo, anti-permits.
- Farrid Adams, slogan-writer.
- S. Malope, 'I'm non-violent.'
- Moses Kotan[e], banned man
- Leon Levy, trade unionist.
- E. Maleie, A.N.C. member.
- Philemon Mathole, A.N.C. member.
- Nimrod Sejake, A.N.C. member.
- Stanley Lollan, S.A.C.P.O. Sec.
- P. P. Nthite, Youth Leaguer.
- Paul Joseph, T.I.C. member.
- P. Beyleveld, C.O.D. chief.
- S. Masemola, glamour-boy.
- Phineas Nen[e], A.N.C. member
- B. Hlapane, A.N.C. member.
- Ida Mntwana, ANC song-leader.
- V. Make, boycotter.
- J.S.A. Mavuso, A.N.C. member.
- T. Musi, Youth Leaguer.
- L. Masina, trade unionist.
- Gert Sibande, "Lion of east."
- W. M. Sisulu, businessman.
- Ronald Press, doctor.
- J. Molefi, boycotter.
- Sydney Shall, medical student.
- E. P. Moretsele, cafe owner.
- Isaac Bokala, A.N.C. member.
- H. G. Makgothi, Youth Leaguer.
- L. Nkosi, trade unionist.
- Peter Selepe, A.N.C. member.
- A. M. Kathrada, banned man.
- A. Hutchinson, teacher.
- T. X. Makiwane, journalist.
- J. Nkadimen[g], trade unionist
- H. M. Moosa, medical doctor.
- J. Hadebe, Youth Leaguer.
- Norman Levy, C.O.D. member.
- Mohamed Asmal, boycotter.
- Lionel Morrison, slogan-writer.
- O. Motsabi, A.N.C. member.
- Cleopas Sibande, clerk.
- July Mashaba, A.N.C. member.
- L. Bernstein, architect.
- Bertha Mash[aba], women's leader
- Simon Tyiki, truck-driver.
- Yetta Barenblatt, C.O.P. Sec.
- J. Modise, Youth Leaguer.
- Suliman Nathie, T.I.C. member.
- D. C. Thompson, priest.
- Hymie Barsel, C.O.D. member.
- Aaron Mahlangu, A.N.C. member.
- Nelson Mandela, lawyer.
- Joseph Kumalo, anti-pass.
- R. Tunzi, electrician.

NTL

- E. Shanley, trade unionist.
- Dorothy Shanley, housewife.
- P. Manana, A.N.C. member.
- J. Arenstein, housewife.
- M. P. Naicker, N.I.C. member.
- Bertha Mkize, expelled.
- K. T. Naicker, N.I.C. member.
- P. G. Mei, A.N.C. member.
- G. M. Naick[er], medical doctor

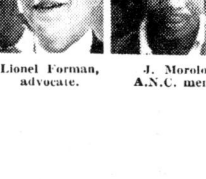

dian Congress.   NTL: Natal.   OFS: Orange Free State.   SACPO: South African Coloured People's Organisation.   TIC: Transvaal Indian Congress.   TVL: Transvaal.

S. Ngcobo, N.C. member. | Billy Nair, N.I.C. member. | J. Hoogendyk, trade unionist. | V. Pillay, N.I.C. member. | M. B. Yengwa, ex-deportee. | N. M. Motala, medical doctor. | A. Gumede, A.N.C. member. | Debi Singh, N.I.C. member. | J. G. Matthews, law student. | G. Hurbans, N.I.C. member.

P. Simelane, N.C. member. | I. C. Meer, lawyer. | S. Dhlamini, A.N.C. member. | D. A. Seedat, N.I.C. member. | Dorothy Nyembe, A.N.C. member. | Kesval Moonsamy, N.I.C. member. | **OFS** | M. Mahlakoane, A.N.C. member. | A. Sechoareng, A.N.C. member. | Gabriel Dichabe, A.N.C. member.

Monnanyana, N.C. member. | J. Mafora, A.N.C. member. | **CP** | J. Mposa, A.N.C. member. | J. A. Calata, priest. | G. Peake, SACPO member. | J. Mtini, A.N.C. member. | D. Mgugunyeka, A.N.C. member. | Alex la Guma, writer. | W. S. Gawe, priest.

Fred Carneson, ex-M.P.C. | T. Tshunungwa, expelled. | F. Matomela, A.N.C. member. | J. Jack, photographer. | C. Jasson, SACPO member. | F. Ntsangani, A.N.C. member. | Joe Nkampeni, A.N.C. member. | E. Mfaxa, A.N.C. member. | T. Tshume, A.N.C. member. | W. Mati, A.N.C. member.

R. Damons, SACPO member. | A. Sibeko, A.N.C. member. | S. Vanqa, A.N.C. member. | Sonia Bunting, housewife. | Asha Dawood, SACPO member. | A. Nogaya, A.N.C. member. | V. Mini, A.N.C. member. | A. E. Letele, medical doctor. | F. Baard, women's leader. | L. B. Lee-Warden, M.P.

L. Kepe, N.C. member. | J. Buza, A.N.C. member. | G. Ngotyana, globe-trotter. | W. Mkwayi, A.N.C. member. | R. September, SACPO member. | P. Mashibini, A.N.C. member. | A. Silinga, A.N.C. member. | Lionel Forman, advocate. | J. Morolong, A.N.C. member. | B. Turok, surveyor.

Simon Nkaliphe, convict. | D. Fuyani, A.N.C. member. | T. Mqota, A.N.C. member. | C. Makhohliso, A.N.C. member. | I. O. Horvitch, architect. | B. Ndimba, A.N.C. member. | C. Mayekiso, A.N.C. member.

All the accused *turn over!*

The four distinguished accused below were once DRUM masterpieces-in-bronze!

A. J. Luthuli, A.N.C. president. | Lilian Ngoyi, women's leader. | W. Z. Conco, medical doctor. | Z. K. Matthews, professor.

The bail conditions forbid the accused to be present at political meetings and compel them to report to the nearest police station once a week

The state produced 10 000 exhibits for the preparatory examination, alleged to have been seized from the organisations to which the accused belonged.

Nelson Mandela and Ruth First outside the Court. The trial brought together leaders from throughout the country. Many had known each other by name only but had never met before.

Helen Joseph, Secretary of the Federation of South African Women, one of the accused, at the Pretoria court in 1958.

Were they paralysed?
During the preparatory examination, they were brought closer together than they had ever been before, in one net: lawyers, medical doctors, lecturers and teachers, clerks, messengers, trade unionists, newspapermen, ministers of religion and others

Drum: September 1957 The long preparatory examination started on 19 December 1956. Under the shadow of the Treason Trial, the leaders of four main organisations were brought together – by force – in one long conference: ANC, SAIC, SACP and the COD, consisting of whites only. They are out on bail but their bail conditions forbid their presence at political meetings and compel them to report to the nearest police station once a week. What does the Crown allege? It alleges that the Freedom Charter, drawn up by the four main organisations making up the 'liberation movement', sets out steps towards the overthrow of

Photographs by Alf Kumalo, Peter Magubane, Gopal Naransamy and Jurgen Schadeberg

Aziz Pahad (second from left), Winnie Mandela and Nelson Mandela (centre) with supporters singing outside the Court in Pretoria in 1958. Ninety-one people faced the actual trial. Sixty-four had been discharged after the preparatory examination had been completed in Johannesburg late in 1957.

the government and the creation of a communist state; that some of the accused made speeches advocating extra-parliamentary action towards this purpose, ie a revolution conducted by means of violence and bloodshed.

One of the defence lawyers, Vernon Berrange QC, argued that the treason alleged against the 156 amounted to a 'political plot' like those trumped up by authorities during the period of the Inquisition or the Reichstag fire trial in Germany. The defence would prove that the accused were 'victims of political kite-flying on the part of those responsible for the prosecutions'. 'This is no ordinary case', he said, 'if one has regard to the crude jackboot manner in which the arrests were affected.' Some members of the Special Branch of the CID admitted under cross-examination by the defence that the ANC had often stressed 'the non-violent nature of its struggle'.

The preparatory examination was completed in September 1957, charges were withdrawn against 64 people, including Oliver Tambo and Chief Luthuli. □

Sophiatown – The move

Sophiatown was different from other black townships in South Africa. People didn't have to get permission to live there and people of all racial backgrounds could buy and own property there. Despite poverty, squalor and violence, Sophiatown was exuberant and alive.

In 1953 the oldest black settlements – Sophiatown, together with three other townships in the western part of Johannesburg – were declared 'blackspots' by the government. The 'blackspots', surrounded by white suburbs, were scheduled for removal.

During 1956, most parts of the Western Areas were proclaimed white group areas

Photographs by Jurgen Schadeberg

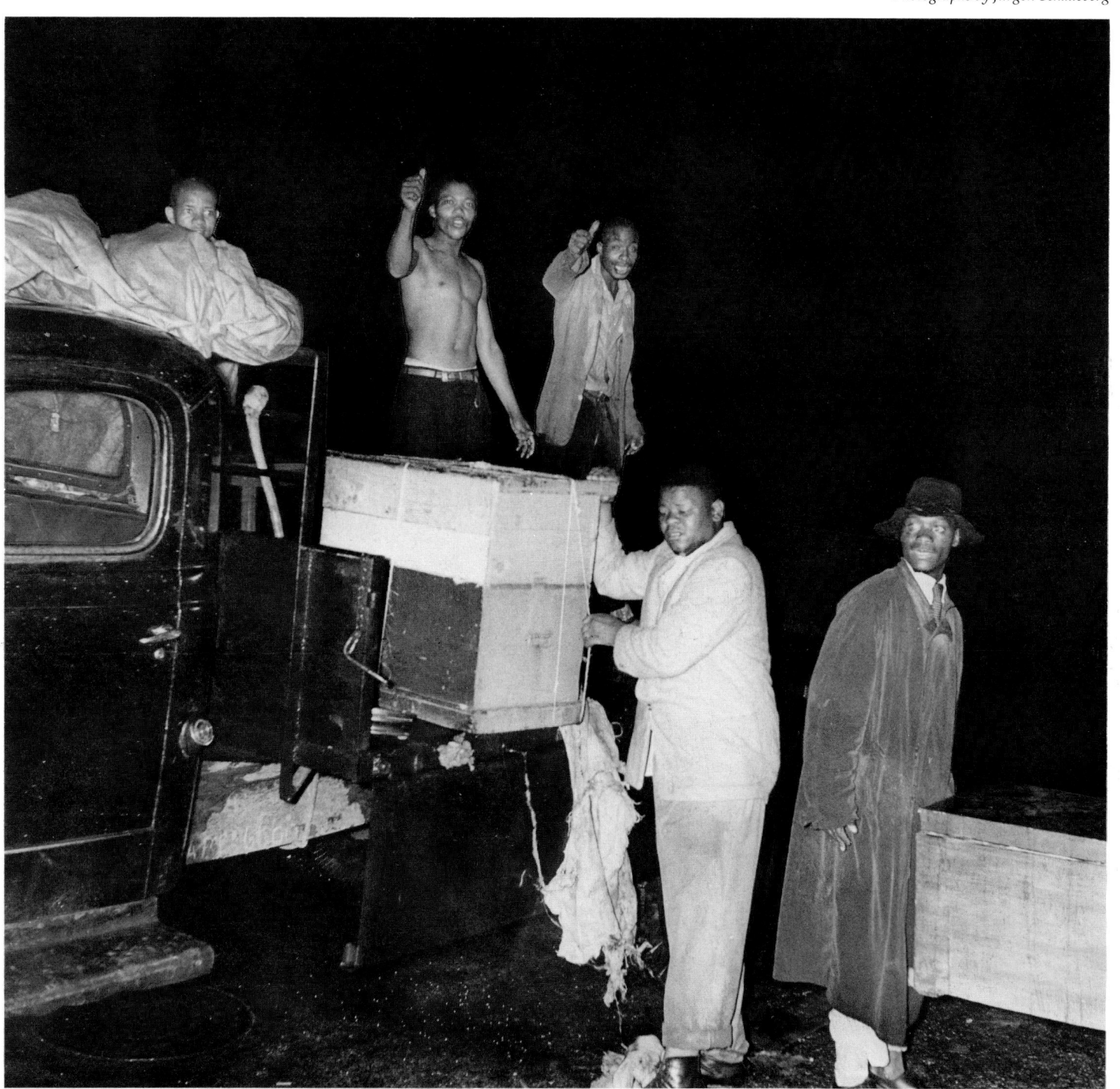

On the night before the surprise Sophiatown move, Congress organiser Steven Segale moved anti-removal families from their homes to St Cyprian's School to avoid the move to Meadowlands. It was done in pouring rain.

Sophiatown removals

12 February 1955 was the day the Sophiatown removals were due to start. The ANC had called 5 000 volunteers to mobilise the people around the slogan of defiance 'Asi hambi – We won't go!' and a stay-away was planned for the first removal day. On 10 February, two days ahead of schedule, eighty lorries and 2 000 armed police moved into Sophiatown and began to move the people out of homes they had occupied for generations.

It took 2 000 armed police and army reinforcements to move the first 100 African families and their belongings to Meadowlands

Photographs by Jurgen Schadeberg

One late night, thousands of armed police moved into Sophiatown.

'Sophiatown, my beloved Sophiatown, the centre of the metropolis'

The best musicians, scholars, educationalists, doctors, laywers, clergymen, singers, artists and politicians came from Sophiatown

Writers, musicians, politicians and journalists live side by side with the gangsters, shebeen queens and black and white 'Bohemians' in Sophiatown. There was the boxer, Ezekiel Dlamini, hero of the jazz opera King Kong. *There was blues singer Dolly Rathebe and, of course,* Drum *editor Can Themba and writer 'Bloke' Modisane, among many others.*

Photographs by Bob Gosani

The families were put in little matchbox houses, four times further from their work than before

120

Photographs by Bob Gosani

In Sophiatown non-working crowds gathered during the day to sing in defiance. Stay-at-home during 1956 was effective in areas like Sophiatown because people's tempers had been pent up in recent months with the removals and permit raids.

Bulldozers – Gutted houses

By 1959 most of the houses in Sophiatown had disappeared. In the background is the tower of St Cyprian's Church of Christ the King.

Last days of Sophiatown

Drum: November 1959 Sophiatown, the city that was within a city, the Gay Paris of Johannesburg, the notorious Casbah gang den, the shebeeniest of them all; Sophiatown is now breathing for the last time.

I was robbed on her streets, beaten up on her dark corners, and I'll never forget the day when a woman friend of mine was grabbed from me by Sophiatown's tough sons. Her people do not like the fact that she is being murdered and I sympathise with them because she was a free city. There were no superintendents who kept files on each household and there were no Black Jacks who could wake you up at 4 am and take you to a location superintendent who comes in at 8.30 am.

There is pathos, mirth, murder and sweet abandon in her past history. Way back in the early thirties, where the Odin Cinema now stands abandoned, was the Undermoon Hall, where African Jazz was born. The young set used to buy dagga from a pedlar opposite the hall, and he hid his stuff in a big tree. This hall was a rough house. Randy dames from nearby suburbs used to come for their entertainment and they caused trouble. Guys used to fight over them, using bicycle chains and knuckle-dusters.

Soon after, gangs sprouted. There were the Cowboys, who controlled a big hunk of Sophiatown, the Black Cops, the Orange and Blacks. Vivian Dladla arrived with his Berlins. The Berlins were the best gang in Sophiatown and they ruled. After the war years came the Americans with Kort Boy, and Chanam, who was sometimes known as the Durango Kid. The former was an expert with a gun, and the latter was a two-gun-toting *hombre*. The last of the gangs in Sophiatown were the Wisbeys and on a wall at the corner of Gibson and Victoria you can see an epitaph to the gangs, reading: 'He who comes to destroy Dead End shall himself be destroyed and that goes for the FBI too.' The FBI are the cops. There are a lot of boys famous in Sophiatown history. There is Boy Malaita, Kort Boy and Fat Boitjie. You find such names as Lefty Tengo because this guy killed Tengo Jabavu, and Lefty Spoiler, because he was a member of the Spoilers. Names like Peter Berlin,

Photographs by Jurgen Schadeberg

Kush Cadillac, and Steele Mercury too. Where the folk excelled was also in naming the shebeens.

There was Aunt Babes, in Edith Street. Bright's Place in Tucker, and opposite him the Carlton Hotel, run by a Chinaman. Then there was the Clubhouse where the guys drank beers and at the same time lifted weights. The House on Telegraph Hill in Milner Street; Back of the Moon at the corner of Gibson and Milner, and the Thirty Nine Steps. Just shows you that they had imagination. This naming craze was only excelled by Can Themba's House of Truth and the House of Saints.

Don't go away with the idea that Sophiatown's population was only composed of the pleasure-loving and the rough. She had her respectable citizens. There was Dr A B Xuma, the African MD, and Mr J R Rathebe, who reminds everybody that he was once in America. Mr B J Mabuza, owner of Benna Court, is still sticking to his place because he can't forget Sophiatown and its charm. And Sophiatown will also boast that she built two gentlemen who fell in love with her – Anthony Sampson and Father Trevor Huddleston – into world figures.

Walking on her streets today she looks like a bombed city. The signs that say 'We Won't Move' stand as a mockery to people who thought they could defend their beloved homes. The few citizens who remain are hounded out of their houses for not possessing permits. Women lock their houses during the day because police demand pass books from them. And today there are hundreds who sleep on verandahs, live with friends, and live in the ruins. The City Council was urged to make a tent town and its answer was to open a red tape office. The rains are coming and they will find many people homeless. Meantime, whites are sleeping snug in two good houses which used to belong to Dr Xuma and to Mr Mannabhay. What can I say? It is not going to make any difference anyhow. □

Benson Dyantyi

And after the people had gone, the demolition squads moved into Sophiatown and levelled it.

Xmas and me: It's a tough, jazzy, dreadful season in my Sophiatown

Drum: December 1955 In my Sophiatown, Christmas insinuates itself on and from 16 December. I become rattled by the constant crack of fireworks. I jump and rush out to see if anybody I know has not been shot. Women scream every night.

I have enough worries of my own. I begin to worry about what the children at home are going to wear; a new suit for each of the two boys, a dress for the little girl. Shoes, socks, hats, shirts and maybe toys. There must be a chicken or turkey and perhaps a bottle or two of brandy.

Christmas Eve, which is also pay-day, I come home laden with gifts, but before I get home I meet a group of people in comic dress singing jazz or pop songs they have made up for the season. Women's bodies bulge disturbingly in men's attire, and men with painted faces and lips, wearing short dresses, walk with an awkward sway. I follow them aimlessly, lured by their song and frolic. I follow them along dirty, twisting streets and through smelly backyards, walking into pools of stagnant water. I find myself miles from home and tappet back to find friends waiting for me.

'Happy Christmas!' they shout, shaking my hand. I'm expected to offer drinks, but past 'dry' Christmases have taught me my lesson and five minutes later they drift out. I can't afford to give everybody a drink. Then the girls walk in. They are lovely, they are happy and distracting, as only African girls can be. I find myself putting a bottle on the table. Jazz trumpets blare in the background as we drink and dance round and round in the room until I collapse.

Then it is Christmas morning. My head is heavy, my tongue is bitter and my body is numb. The streets become swarmed with merrymakers carrying drinks, because nobody gets arrested on Christmas. Girls wearing trousers shout: 'Happy!' Cars speed wildly along the narrow streets, forcing us into the gutters. The filth from the gutter is laughed off. Somewhere along the way we find a little girl's body on the side of the gutter. She was unlucky.

We meet other groups, exchange drinks and greetings. We go up one street and witness a fight. Four hoodlums

Big machines and men with picks are beating down the last walls of Sof'town. Take a last look and say goodbye.

Photographs by Jurgen Schadeberg

are stabbing one man. He tries to break away from them and run for it, but they stay with him, their blades sinking into his body until he falls. One of the four 'heroes' kicks the fallen man in the face, and they walk off brandishing their blades and threatening to stab anybody who gets in their way. The sight of a man dying always fills me with horror. I get our group to walk off.

Somewhere on our way a woman screams and complains that a certain man wants to drag her away by force. We turn round to face the man and find ourselves confronted by a hostile gang of armed thugs. The girls scream and rush in all directions. Some of us get stabbed. Then I walk home. Dejected.

Ambulances stream past with frightful regularity. The groups become fewer, the wails of women long and frequent, and I shut my door and feel sorry for the race of man and for being part of it. The greatest killer in the locations is the season of Christmas, and one day I dread to look at the newspapers is the day after Christmas.

But in my mind I know there should be a Christmas away from the crowded streets, the smelling gutters and the killing animals who cannot be happy without causing misery. It will be full of good cheer. Perhaps I am a dreamer. If so, then I never want to wake and find myself with the Christmases I know. □

William 'Bloke' Modisane

World's longest walk to work

Drum: March 1957 Azikhwelwa! For all its fierce passion and aggressive power, this slogan of the bus boycott in Johannesburg and Pretoria is in the passive voice. The passive voice form expresses the mute long suffering and frustration of a voiceless people. But more, much more. It is the cry of a caged animal trying to find a way out.

The bus firm, Putco, had a case. Increased running costs, increased wages had made it impossible for it to continue operating the bus systems without increasing fares. Then suddenly 7 January was upon us. The day of the increased fares. And the boycott was on. Grim-set people walked nine miles to work and nine miles back to their homes in Alexandra. Sophiatowners walked gaily, chattily.

That spark of hope, of strength, is the true cause lying underneath the implacable spirit of Alexander the Great! The boycott is 100 per cent, and the spirit it engenders is getting more so.

The boycotters walked on. They slogged up the hills. They slushed through the rain. They shouted 'Azikhwelwa!' (The buses shall not be boarded.) Then came the sympathy boycotts. Moroka, George Goch and Randfontein joined in. Commerce met, but would not discuss wage increases. Check! The people met, but would not give up the boycott. Check! The police came, but could not break the boycott. Check! The matter was discussed in Parliament, but the government would not give way, no matter whether the boycott lasted a month or six months. Stalemate! □

Can Themba

The Cape bus boycott took deep and violent breaths for about two weeks and fizzled out in the following week. Mr A la Guma, Chairman of the Cape Branch of the South African Coloured People's Organisation, said when the boycott came to a close that he and his committee were satisfied that the bulk of the non-Europeans in the Peninsula were against apartheid.

'Azikhwelwa! Hadipalangoe! Don't ride 'em!'

The ANC was testing its strength. The boycott went on and on and on, on foot, on bicycles, on horse-drawn carts, in taxis, in cars of sympathisers, in vans and lorries

In Port Elizabeth they boycotted the buses and walked to work.

Don't buy tickets for apartheid! Don't boycott the boycott!

Along Louis Botha Avenue the police stopped cars and lorries which gave lifts to Africans and asked for passes and tax receipts. Police warned white motorists that giving lifts was unauthorised.

Protest and bannings

The 1958 'Stay-at-home' strike was called for three days from 26 June, the anniversary of the second 1950 stay-away and the opening of the Defiance Campaign. The two main slogans were '£1 a day' and 'The Nats must go'.

6 December 1957 Idealist Rev Blaxall during the multi-racial conference which was appropriately held in the learned halls of the University of the Witwatersrand. The conference promised co-operation and sweet reasonableness.

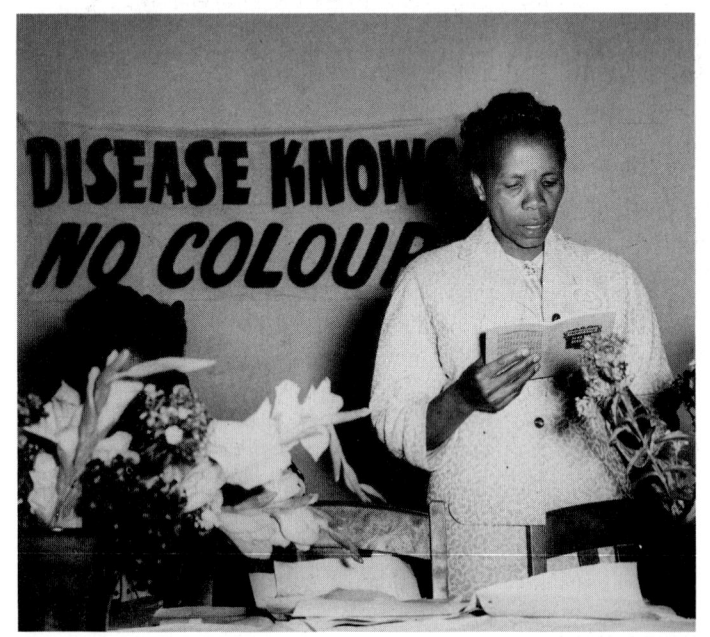

Drum: January 1958 *Voices of non-white nurses rang out far and clear when nursing apartheid became law. They refused to be advised or controlled by white nurses. So they called a conference in Johannesburg and set up a new all-race group, the Federation of South African Nurses and Midwives. They will try to gain affiliation with the International Council of Nurses.*

The ban on Congress

Drum: May 1958 What hath the ban of the African National Congress in parts of the Marico district – which includes Zeerust – and the Soutpansberg district of the Transvaal wrought? The ban that says Congress property in these areas may be destroyed or sold.

It makes Congress officials or members liable to a maximum fine of £300 and up to three years' imprisonment, or both, if they don't resign. Similar sentences for abetters and obstructors. Similar sentences for the display or utterance of Congress slogans, or the making of Congress signs, or for contributing to Congress funds, or for interfering with officials who want to see the law get tough about its regulations. And it doesn't matter nothing if the Congress changes its name. Whew!

It has not sent a shudder of apprehension through the ANC in the whole country. It has not sent a tingle of new confidence through those whites who have been made to feel there's a sinister menace in their kitchens and backyards. Above all, it has not relieved the tension in that haywire town of Zeerust and its environs. But it has given the Congress a name and a local habitation. Before the troubles in Marico, Congress was a remote thing there. Men did not go to the town court in hundreds. Women did not politicise, talk of 'this government', 'those Europeans'. Tribal areas all over the Union dreamed away an unperturbed life, people tilling the lands, minding the stock. Later, men began to lift the thumb, bark 'Afrika!' and feel they were one with those 'inflammatories' in Johannesburg.

People who are not Congressites now speak Congress language, think of all forms of protest through a Congress heart. I have seen a black driver swearing it out with a white driver, like drivers all over the world, and a few bystanders have shouted 'Afrika!' when it seemed that the African had worsted the white man in the verbal joust. Africans – tribal Africans mostly – like greeting: 'Thama Kgosi' – Hail, my lord – in the Northern Transvaal; 'Molo' – (Good) morning – in Xhosaland; 'Sa'ubona' – We greet you – in Zululand. But now in the politically-charged *lingua franca*, they all greet each other with the thumbs-up sign and the thunderous 'Afrika!' with the standard reply, 'Iyabuya!' – She'll come back.

These things have the deepest political significance. They must be linked with movements such as the Defiance Campaign, the anti-pass campaigns, the sullen resistance of squatters, the bus boycott, the grim future. But now, because of the threat to the Congress, Africans all over are looking for 'other' political weapons. Economic boycott? Underground movements? Infiltration into official and police ranks? Alliance with other races? I have heard it said: 'They can only ban us to where we'll burrow tunnels under their high-mindedness.' And I have heard it said:

Congressites give the thumbs-up sign – now banned in some areas – at a Jo'burg meeting which decided on protest action.

'The troubles of those country people are the troubles of every non-white.'

This ban is likely to serve only extremism, to deprive the people of the responsible and stabilising influence of the Congress in some areas. This has been wrought by the powers, for 'peace, order and good government'. □

Can Themba

Africanists cut loose at Transvaal ANC meeting

On the first day, in open conference, big-voiced Africanist, Peter Motsele, says: 'President asks us to co-operate with apartheidists. We want no co-operation with the whites at this stage'. His followers stamp their feet. But there are just as many people who sit grim and silent.

Drum: 1 November 1958 The threat of rain in the air; of political uproar in the area. We wait impatiently outside the Sekgapa-madi (Blood-spilling) Hall in Orlando, Johannesburg, where many a bloody Congress fight has broken out in the past. Dramatic things are expected at this conference of the Transvaal branch of the African National Congress. For months the Africanists, the nationalist wing of the Congress, have been organising a putsch to oust the Freedom Chartership leaders of the ANC in the province. This is to be the first step towards grabbing control of the National Executive.

It is about 3.30, and we go into the hall. In row upon row sit the Congressites. On the stage are Oliver Tambo, suave Johannesburg lawyer, acting as chairman; portly Chief Luthuli, National President-General; Y Puthini, National President of the Youth League. Chief Luthuli gives the presidential address. He makes calculated jabs at apartheid; how it had deteriorated race relations. But he says that we Africans should not emulate that way of thinking and follow a narrow nationalism. We should co-operate with the whites.

During his speech a horde of Africanists enter the hall at the back, to the booming sounds of heavy boots. With their coming, the atmosphere is galvanised into high tension. Mr Z Mothopeng is the first speaker. He says that he doesn't care about the multiracial society. In this country the people are divided into two groups only: the oppressors and the oppressed. There can be no co-operation with the oppressors. Then speaker after speaker makes the points: This presidential address asks us to co-operate with apartheidists. We don't accept whites at this stage. Let us not forget our origins; we shall consider co-operation when we have come into our own first.

Sunday, 2 November. Tension is still in the air, but a vital change has been wrought overnight. Scores of young men are milling about, openly wielding sticks, clubs and sjamboks. The Charterists have rallied their own strong-arm men 'to resist Africanist force with force', and these men are guarding the conference, still in closed session. A little further away a group of Africanists stand ruefully. Now and then a knobkerrie charge, and some Africanist flees for his life. □

Can Themba

It was one of the stormiest conferences for many a day. Tempers flared, sticks were brandished. But it was not violence which made the drama. The high moment, the real tension came with the decision of the Africanists to split from the Transvaal Congress

Photographs by Peter Magubane

Peter Molotsi, later to become PAC Secretary, from the back of the hall: 'We have to protect our national identity, our customs, our traditions, and the communists just want to overwhelm us.'

Bus boycott leader, Josias Madzunya, fiery Africanist, tells delegates: 'We are concerned with the liberation of Africans. God has created Europe for the Europeans and Asia for the Asians.

Barred from the hall: Rosette Ndziba says there is no such thing as 'narrow nationalism'. 'The Freedom Charter and this recent talk of racial co-operation is just to fool you.' He is later kept out of the hall.

Robert Sobukwe, Witwatersrand University lecturer and chief Africanist theoretician, declaims: 'We shall think of co-operation with other races when we have come into our own.'

131

The women of Cato Manor act

In Cato Manor (for more background see page 168) following a mild outbreak of typhoid, steps were taken to clear up the unsanitary conditions. Stills and drums of home-brewed beer were destroyed by the police and municipal workers. This affected a large group of women who brewed traditional beer. There was a restriction on home brewing, which enabled the Durban Corporation to draw a large revenue from its beer halls, where all the social drinking now took place.

On 17 June 1959 the first beer hall was invaded by an army of furious women; its male customers were driven outside, beer vats were overturned and brewing machinery was destroyed

Photographs by G R Naidoo

Hounded women of slum Cato Manor, Durban, strapped babies to their backs, took up sticks to protest against the way they were treated and the way they had to live. One day two people were shot. Many were injured. Buildings were gutted. Above right, defence attorney Rowley Arenstein, a Congress of Democrats activist, carried up high by the women.

For two weeks the women expressed their anger in demonstrations, invasions of beer halls, and clashes with the police, and with ANC support some beer halls were burnt to the ground and others were picketed.

Cape Town welcomes Luthuli

Congress policy is for a multi-racial society in which all races will have a place

Drum: June 1959 'Somlandela Luthuli! – We will follow Luthuli!' These words were sung loudly and often by thousands and thousands of people in Cape Town recently during a triumphant visit by Chief Albert Luthuli, President-General of the African National Congress.

On Sunday morning the song shook the roof of Cape Town's station as a train brought the beaming, round-faced Chief into the middle of a crowd of Congress supporters (and Special Branch policemen). There was much cheering, lifting of thumbs and shaking of hands by the Congress supporters. Then they went out into the sunshine of the Grand Parade, where a Guard of Honour of uniformed Volunteers stood surrounded by several hundred people.

'Somlandela Luthuli.'

The Chief looked up at the mountain towering over Cape Town. 'I have often read,' he said, 'that General Smuts gained inspiration from Table Mountain. I don't know what sort of inspiration it was – but it certainly did not do our people much good. I hope I shall get a different sort of inspiration, the inspiration to work towards a democratic, multi-racial South Africa.' But by the end of his visit, it turned out that it was not the mountain, but the people of Cape Town, who inspired Luthuli. In turn, they were inspired by him.

When Chief Luthuli strode into the Drill Hall that Sunday afternoon, he found himself addressing the biggest indoor political meeting ever held in the city. Two thousand people filled the hall. 'Afrika, Mayibuye! Somlandela Luthuli!' shouted the crowd.

An African trade unionist popped up onto the platform and put a garland of ferns around the Chief's neck. Luthuli got up to make a speech. 'The challenge you see is this: For how long will the oppressor carry on? For how long will Mother Africa and her sons and daughters be forced to suffer under tyranny?' he asked the crowd.

'Nigeria is to be free in 1960, and perhaps if the younger people were more serious about the freedom struggle, we too might well enjoy freedom in 1960 . . . I like to believe that the powers-that-be reserved South Africa to be a place where race relations could be worked out for the benefit of the whole world.

'I say this generation is fortunate – fortunate to be able to surrender itself fully to a struggle. My message to Cape Town is this: That this generation should say to itself, "I shall perish if need be for Africa!" This is your home – if you use it. Afrika! Mayibuye!" The crowd rose to its feet to sing both the Luthuli song and 'Nkosi Sikelele Afrika' before the uniformed guards escorted the Chief away.

Luthuli's other big meeting during his four-day visit took place in the Rondebosch Town Hall and was designed to allow whites to hear the Chief. The Town Hall is meant to hold only about 600 people. More than 1 000 pushed themselves in. About 500 of these were whites. There they were, densely packed, in the aisles and along the sides. Mixed.

Luthuli's subject was 'European fears and non-white aspirations'. He said the non-white aspirations were for freedom and democracy. This they hoped to achieve by extra-parliamentary non-violent methods. He mentioned the present programme of boycotting Nationalist goods and intensifying the anti-pass struggle. As for European fears, he repeated that Congress policy was for a multi-racial society in which all races would have a place. The whites in the audience looked a little surprised – and even startled – at the singing and shouting that began and ended the meeting. But they listened to the Chief's long and closely-thought-out speech with rapt attention. No one barracked or interrupted, and no one asked any unfriendly questions. At the end one white man got up to congratulate Luthuli on the dignity and sincerity with which he had spoken.

Chief Luthuli said afterwards that he had never addressed a meeting quite like this before. He thought such meetings could only happen in the Cape. In Durban, of course, he often had white people at his meetings, but they were usually only a few, committed Congress supporters. He had never had a whole hall full of ordinary, non-political whites sitting among Africans.

The next day the Chief attended a debate in Parliament and saw students and Black Sash women who were demonstrating outside. After he came out, an unknown Afrikaner from the country, who had also listened to the debate, came and shook Luthuli's hand and said: 'I apologise for the things my people are doing in there'. In four days Luthuli had conquered Cape Town. By the time his train pulled out of the station again, the chant that had greeted him had become the hit tune of the town.

'Somlandela Luthuli! We will follow Luthuli!' □

Kenneth Mackenzie

'We could be free in 1960, too, if the younger folk took their politics more seriously. This could be your hour'

Photograph by Ranjith Kally

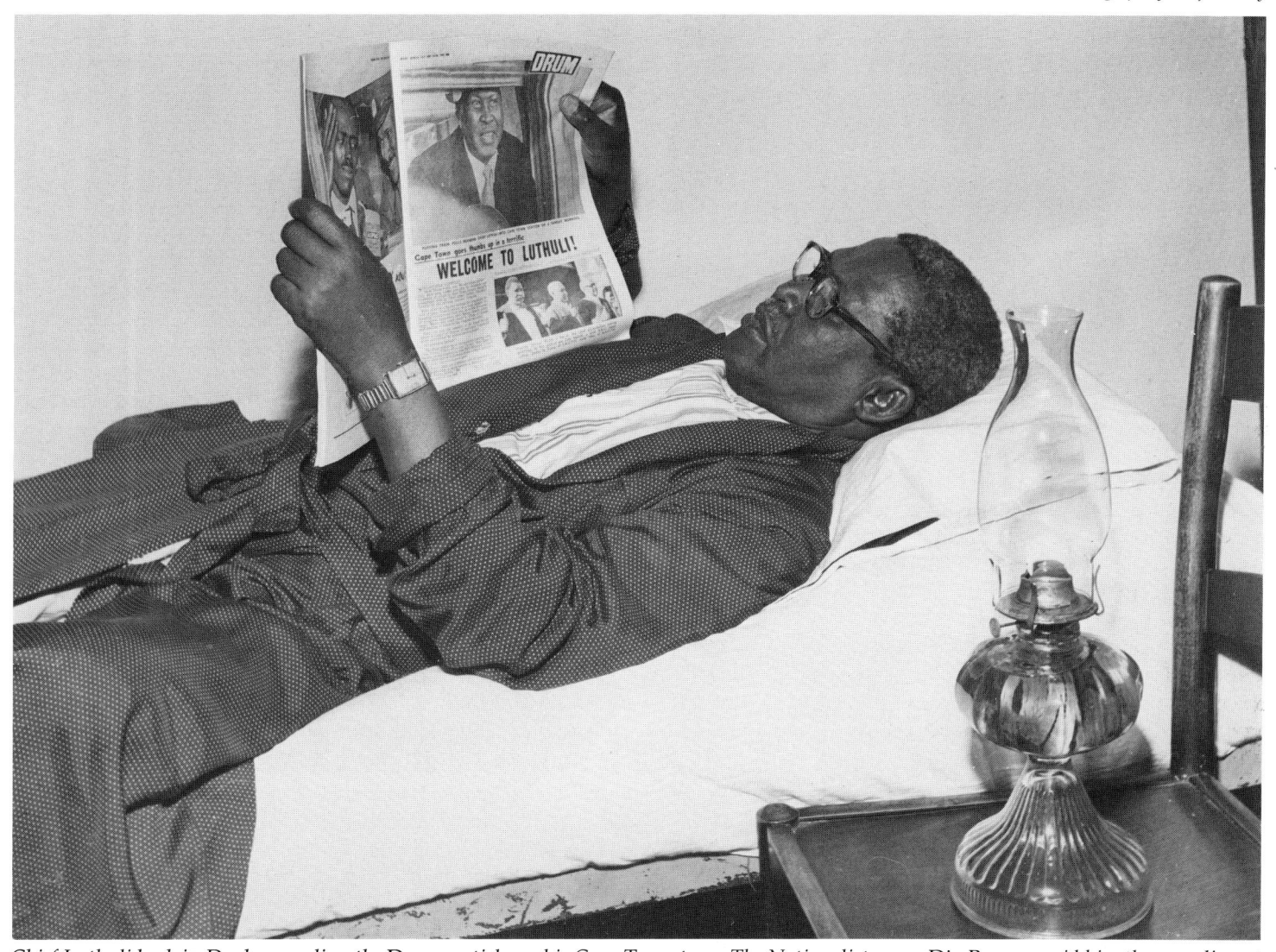

Chief Luthuli back in Durban reading the Drum *article on his Cape Town tour. The Nationalist paper* Die Burger *paid him the compliment of printing a long attack on him and his boycott proposals.*

Non-political whites turned up in hundreds to see Luthuli, hear his views at the multi-racial meeting. 'I thought it could only happen in the Cape,' said Luthuli

Praying women of Ixopo

Five hundred women went to see the government, carrying a white flag and a banner which said: 'The grievances of the women'. As they walked, they were silent.

The Ixopo women marched to put their grievances to the government. They took a white flag to show they went in peace. But they never went home that night. Somebody broke their flag and threw it on the ground, and the women ended that day of prayer in jail

Drum: November 1959 They gathered one day from eleven districts surrounding the Ixopo magisterial area. They marched in silence through the town to the Magistrate's Office, carrying a white flag and a sign reading: 'The grievances of the women'.

They had seen the Native Commissioner of the area, Mr F W Beyer, two months before, and had presented him with a list of their grievances. They asked that he investigate their complaints and make representations on their behalf. The women said that he had asked them to call and receive a reply to their requests after two months.

But the women were told by Mr Beyer that he was not prepared to discuss their complaints, and that they should report to their husbands, who should in turn report to the chiefs. Mr Beyer was only prepared to grant an audience to the chiefs. The women did not accept this. They remained squatting outside the offices of the Native Commissioner and said that they would not leave until they had some reply to their questions. While they sat outside the court they recited prayers.

The women prayed while the Captain looked at his watch

Photographs by G R Naidoo

After the women had refused to disperse, they were arrested and all locked up in the police cells.

Then the police came. The squad from Maritzburg was under the command of Captain Edgar Francis Berry Jackson. Tall, powerfully built Captain Jackson strode up to the group of silent women and warned them that their gathering was illegal and that they should disperse within ten minutes. Captain Jackson looked at his watch as the seconds ticked by. Court officials also looked at watches nervously.

The atmosphere was electric. There was complete silence from the women. The Captain, after a few minutes, gave a second warning to the women. Five minutes to go. Suddenly the silent women burst into prayer. Policemen armed with pick handles, small arms, two with Sten guns, and one with a sjambok, stood watching them pray.

They were still praying when the time limit expired. The Captain waited until the prayer was over, and arrested the women. Singing, the women were led into a courtyard under strong police guard. A plainclothes policeman picked up the white flag and held it in his hand. Then he tore off the flag, and kept the stick. Another policeman broke the piece of wood holding the sign which the women had carried. A third policeman picked up a bottle, broke it against a stone, and walked about flourishing the jagged neck.

The women were charged. It was getting dark. Flickering torches gave light to the open-air court. It was cold. The women were found guilty under the Native Code at 12.45 am. The sentence was four months in jail or a £35 fine each. Notice of appeal was lodged. The women were ushered into the waiting buses, and driven off to jail. □

G R Naidoo

On Monday, 21 March 1960, we launch our positive, decisive campaign against pass laws – Robert Sobukwe

There is a new name in the political melting pot: Robert Mangaliso Sobukwe (centre), with his lieutenant, Rosette Ndziba (left) and Unionist Mr Nyaose (right).

Drum: May 1960 A few weeks ago the name Robert Mangaliso – it means 'wonderful' – Sobukwe meant little to people outside the inner circle of African politics here. Today the tall, suave, 35-year-old Witwatersrand University lecturer has become a man with a hand on the strings of political destiny. Until April, Mangaliso was moving quietly behind the political scene, arguing, persuading, organising on behalf of the forces of Africanism which split last year from the African National Congress. Then, all of a sudden, he was catapulted into the headlines with his election as the first president of the new Pan-Africanist Congress, whose cry is 'Africa for the Africans'.

In December 1959, both the ANC and the PAC announced their plan to demonstrate against the pass laws on 31 March 1960. On 4 March, Robert Sobukwe sent out final instructions for the campaign to the PAC branches and Executives. Then, on 18 March, Robert Sobukwe announced that the PAC would now begin the campaign against the pass laws on Monday, 21 March, and called on all Africans to leave their passes at home and surrender to the police. □

'For many months the Pan-Africanist leaders in South Africa had planned a non-violent campaign against the pass laws. We were inspired in this campaign by our brilliant leader, Mangaliso Sobukwe. Our plan of action was that we would deliberately leave our pass books at home, and march in our thousands to the police stations to demand arrest. We would ask no bail, pay no fine. The national working committee finally decided the date of action. It was 21 March 1960'

Philip Kgosana

The Sharpeville killings

Photograph by Ian Berry

Outside Sharpeville police station: a curious crowd. Police open fire. Everyone flees. Some smile.

How it began: 21 March 1960

The crowds seemed to be loosely gathered around the Saracens. The kids were playing. In all there were about 3 000 people. They seemed amiable. Suddenly there was a sharp report from the direction of the police station. There were shrill cries of 'Izwe lethu' (our land) – women's voices, I thought. The cries came from the police station, and I could see a small section of the crowd swirl around the Saracens. Hands went up in the Africanist salute. Then the shooting started. We heard the chatter of a machine gun, then another, then another. There were hundreds of women, some of them laughing. They must have thought the police were firing blanks. One woman was hit about ten yards from our car. Her companion, a young man, went back when she fell. He thought she had stumbled. Then he turned her over and found that her chest had been shot away. He looked at the blood on his hand and said: 'My God, she's gone!'

Hundreds of kids were running too. One little boy had an old blanket coat, which he held up behind his head, thinking, perhaps, that it might save him from the bullets. Some of the children, hardly as tall as the grass, were leaping like rabbits. Some were shot too. Still the shooting went on. One of the policemen was standing on top of a Saracen, and it looked as though he was firing his Sten gun into the crowd. He was swinging it around in a wide arc from his hip as though he was panning a movie camera. Two other police officers were on the track with him, and it looked as if they were firing pistols.

Most of the bodies were strewn on the road running through the field where we were. One man who had been lying still, dazedly got to his feet, staggered a few yards, then fell in a heap. One by one the guns stopped. More than 200 Africans were shot down. The police said that the crowd was armed with 'ferocious weapons' which littered the compound after they fled. I saw no weapons. I saw only shoes, hats and a few bicycles left among the bodies.

Humphrey Tyler, May 1960

They still did not know what was happening. Policemen were standing on top of and beside the Saracens. Some were firing. People's first reaction was to flee, though they did not yet realise the danger.

Photograph by Ian Berry

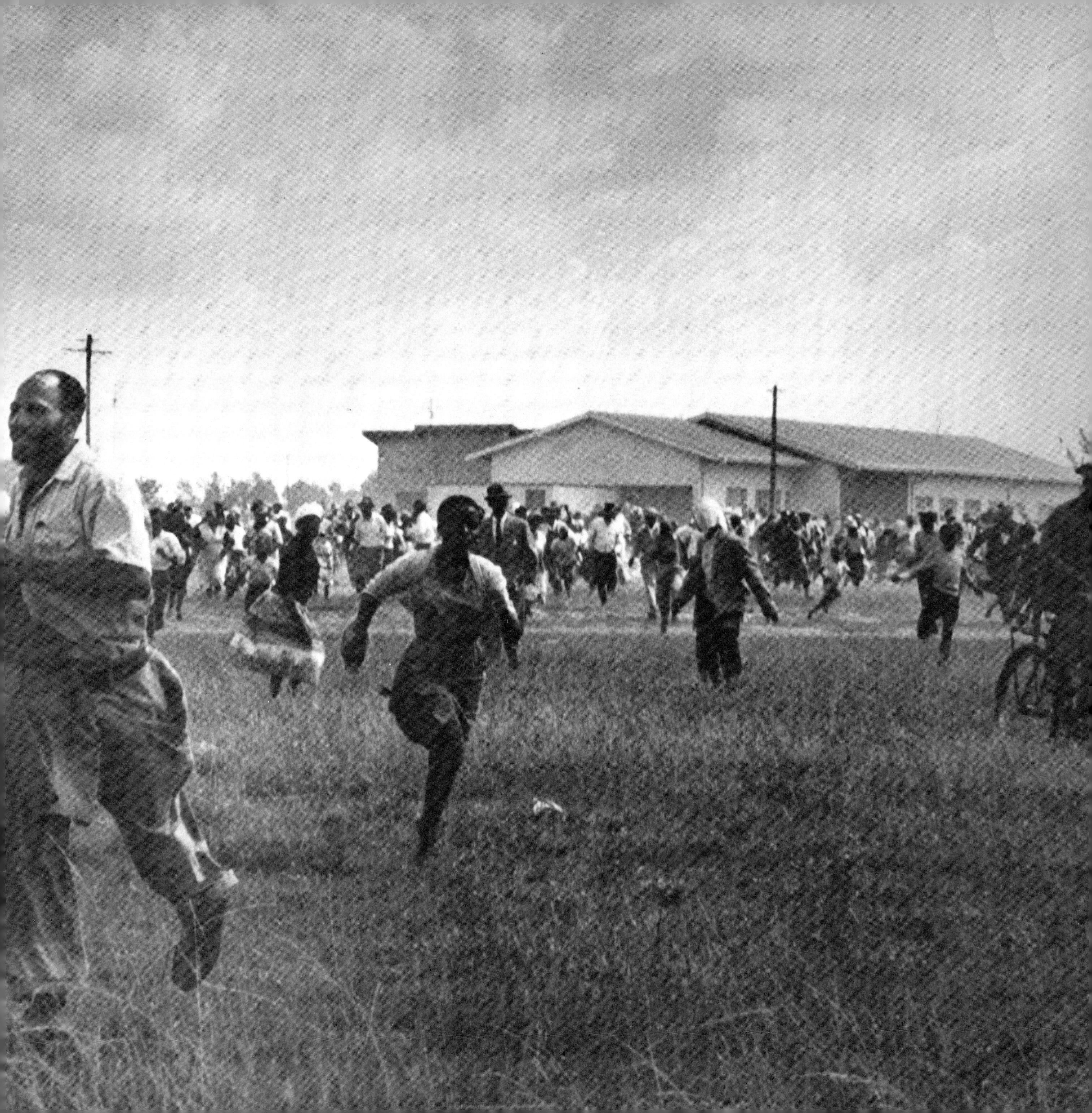

Dead and wounded litter the ground

A few minutes after the shooting came the sudden realisation of what it meant. People found their friends and relatives dead. Some of them were horribly mangled by bullets

Like a ghastly dream; but this had really happened.

67 lay dead, most of them shot in the back; 186 were wounded

Drum: October 1960 'This is the call the African people have been waiting for! It has come! On Monday, 21 March 1960, we launch our positive, decisive campaign against the pass laws in this our country.' Thus spoke Mangaliso Sobukwe three days before Sharpeville. South Africa had started a new phase in her history.

Three days later the Pan-Africanist leaders started their non-violent campaign to reverse apartheid. Mangaliso Sobukwe made his intention clear in a letter to the Commissioner of Police: 'I have given strict instructions,' he said, 'not only to members of my own organisation but also to the African people in general, that they should not allow themselves to be provoked into violent action by anyone.'

The Langa shooting

144

'It was a time of infinite hope and possibility; it seemed not extravagant in the least to predict that the Nationalist government would collapse . . . it was a time of trust, never withdrawal,' writes Lewis Nkosi in Drum

Photograph by Cloete Breytenbach

And so, on the appointed day, Monday, 21 March, thousands of Pan-Africanists reported to the police without their passes and asked to be arrested. Their object was to demonstrate the force of organised non-violence. They wanted to make the pass laws unworkable as a first step in a long campaign to achieve 'freedom and independence' for Africans by 1963.

The police were taken unawares by the crowds of volunteers who asked to be arrested. In some places the leaders were detained, in others they were persuaded to return home. Everything went according to plan, and then, at Sharpeville, tragedy occurred.

At the time of writing, South Africa is still waiting for Mr Justice Wessels, the judge at the judicial enquiry, to report what actually happened at Sharpeville. But the results of the shooting are well known. It was officially announced that 67 Africans were killed and 186 wounded after the police had opened fire on the crowd.

On the same day a riot took place at Langa location near Cape Town, where another crowd of Africans, estimated at 20 000, assembled at police stations to give themselves up for arrest. The police failed to disperse the crowd by baton charges, and the crowd began to throw stones. The police opened fire; two people were killed and 54 were injured.

On the same day, 21 March, 6 000 people gathered outside the Langa police station. After giving a command to disperse, the police made two baton charges on the crowd. Some people started stoning the police and a large crowd surged forward. The commanding officer ordered his men to fire. Two people were killed.

Everywhere they marched. A huge column of men advanced on Durban

South Africa was stunned by the events of Black Monday. The world recoiled in horror, and foreign journalists poured in by every plane. There had been determined action by African nationalists and it had been met with force. It was much more than a riot. More than sixty-seven people died in one day. Inside South Africa prominent men, church and political leaders, expressed their horror. People of all races were shocked, and Africans reacted immediately in many places by staying away from work. African leaders hoped that a stay-at-home would finally persuade white South Africans to press their government for rapid reforms.

Though it was the PAC that took the lead in the anti-pass campaign, it was Chief Luthuli of the ANC who called on Africans to observe 28 March as a day of mourning. PAC leaders supported this move, and Africans responded with unanimity.

The stay-at-home was estimated to have been 95% successful in Cape Town, and between 85% and 95% successful in Johannesburg and Port Elizabeth. Durban was the only main centre where there was little reaction. There were certainly intimidators who bullied some Africans who wanted to work, but could they have bullied almost the whole of Johannesburg and Cape Town's black popula-

Photographs by Ranjith Kally

On 31 March a huge column of men attempted to march from Cato Manor to Durban city centre. The marchers were intercepted by police and driven back. One group of more than a thousand people succeeded in getting through the police cordon and marched through Durban's shopping area, ending up outside the Central Prison demanding the release of detained ANC leaders.

tion? For a brief moment, Africans appeared to have the initiative. The government was caught unawares by their sudden, angry reaction. The pass laws were momentarily relaxed. The people rejoiced in the strength and determination of the new-found leader, Mangaliso Sobukwe, who had resigned his comfortable lectureship at Witwatersrand University and had chosen to lead his followers to prison.

There was a short time in which all Africans were elated. Passes were left at home. They were burnt in piles. Many believed they would never be forced to carry passes again. But this did not last. Just as the African leaders were beginning to believe that their sudden swift campaign had been successful, the government retaliated.

It was round 2.30 am on the morning of 30 March. Detectives and armed police hammered on the doors of hundreds of houses. It was the same in the plush white suburbs and in the townships. Policemen with their lists of wanted people, squad cars on the roads outside. An extraordinary Government Gazette officially declared a State of Emergency. Hundreds of detainees were taken to prison. They came from all walks of life, all races, all income groups, all parts of the country and all political parties. There were gasps of astonishment in Parliament on 22 April when Mr Erasmus, Minister of Defence,

There have been many campaigns against pass laws in South Africa, but none so confident of success.

Pass arrests are suspended – and many passes burned

announced that no less than 1 569 (ninety-four whites, twenty-four coloureds and 1 451 Africans) had been detained. More arrests were to follow, and by 16 May the number had risen to 1 907 detainees who could be jailed for the duration of the Emergency without being charged or tried.

It has been suggested that all the detainees were politically conscious opponents of the government, but some claimed they had never been active in politics. Others had played no active part in politics for ten, twelve or fifteen years. The government, which had temporarily lost the political initiative, soon regained it when almost all the men and women who opposed it were detained, or fled the country.

Many Pan-Africanist leaders were put on trial rapidly for various offences. Sobukwe got £300 or three years' imprisonment for incitement. Matthew Nkoana and 142 others got £300 or three years' imprisonment for not carrying reference books. Almost all the African political leaders were removed from the scene. But this did not satisfy the government, which rushed a bill through Parliament under which both the ANC and PAC were banned on 8 April.

Once the Emergency was declared, things became

8 April 1960 – ANC banned

Photograph by Jurgen Schadeberg

A State of Emergency was declared, and the Army moved into the centre of Johannesburg.

quiet rapidly. The question was, what was the government going to do to prevent this kind of thing from happening again? There were even members of the Nationalist Party who felt that their policies should never be allowed to lead to results like Sharpeville and Langa. They were genuinely astonished by the reaction of the Africans, and hated the use of force.

These Nationalists felt that some form of contact should be established with African leaders. This was the kind of feeling that was reflected by Mr Sauer in his speech at Humansdorp, in which he called for a New Deal and said that, after Sharpeville, conditions in South Africa could never be the same again.

As April drew on, law and order was effectively restored, further stay-aways collapsed, the members of the defence force were given indefinite leave, and the government recovered its confidence. All opposition parties, and the world outside, gave the government constructive advice on the way South Africa could avoid such a tragedy in the future.

What a golden opportunity was presented! And how it was ignored. The government soon showed that it had no intention whatsoever of changing the fundamental principles of *baasskap* and apartheid. On 23 March, two days

Photographs by Ranjith Kally

Thousands of women demonstrated against the State of Emergency and the detention of some 20 000 people, and then were themselves arrested.

after Sharpeville, Dr Verwoerd said, 'We will see to it that we remain in power in this white South Africa'. 'Honest and muscular apartheid will do the trick,' said Mr De Wet Nel. Mr Maree, Minister of Bantu Education, said the solution was to go forward faster than ever before with apartheid.

The Emergency dragged on needlessly for 156 days. Press freedom was restricted. Not only were politicians kept in detention, but gradually people became aware that the Emergency was being used to hold ordinary men who were accused of being 'tsotsis, idlers and loafers'. At one time it was admitted that up to 21 000 were being held at

At the Sharpeville funeral. A voice breaks the silence. 'The Lord has given, and the Lord has taken away,' the Rev Z M Voyi, of the Anglican Church intones.   *Photograph by Jurgen Schadeberg*

Modder B and other detention camps.

In case there should be any more demonstrations, the precaution was taken to reorganise the whole of the South African Defence Force. Not only has the ordinary police force been streamlined, but plans are being made to set up sentinel platoons (*brandwagpelotons*) who could work with the local commandos and be available for action at all times.

Sharpeville might never have happened as far as government policy is concerned. The only difference is that it is now prepared to act tougher than ever before. It has reorganised its security forces, banned African organisations, and imprisoned African leaders, but it has failed to tackle the causes of discontent.

After the people's protest; after the Sharpeville killings; after 20 000 people had been detained; after 156 days of nightmare, the government closed another chapter in our country's history. There was to be no change. Apartheid and *baasskap* were here to stay.

Alan Rake

30 000 obeyed me as one man

Philip Kgosana (in shorts) burst like a bombshell onto the political scene when he led 30 000 people in the famous march on Cape Town. After a powerful demonstration he led the marchers away again without a brick being thrown or a shot fired in anger.

Drum: March 1961 The national working committee finally decided on the date of action – 21 March. To me fell the great honour of making the announcement in the Cape.

'Sons and daughters of the soil, tomorrow we launch our positive, decisive action against the pass laws. How long shall we rot physically, spiritually and morally? How long shall we starve amidst plenty in our fatherland? How long shall we be a rightless, voteless and voiceless majority in our fatherland? We are either slaves or free men.' I went on to quote from Mr Sobukwe's final instructions: 'The only people who will benefit from violence are the police and the government . . . we are fighting for the noblest cause on earth – the liberation of mankind.'

When dawn broke, it was raining. As early as 4.30 am there were 4 000 men in a crowd at the Langa New Flats. I moved from group to group, telling them that we would lead them at 7 am to the Langa police station. The crowd was visibly swelling. By 6 am it had grown to about 10 000 excited men. Then the police came. The atmosphere was tense. I said: 'Gentlemen, we are gathered here to

Philip Kgosana tells of the march of 30 000, with himself at the head, from the township to Cape Town

surrender ourselves for arrest for being without reference books.' My questioner grinned at me. He said: 'You delivered a sensible speech yesterday, but if you attempt to march, then we will defend the police station to the last drop of our blood.' I said: 'Thanks for the warning. Now we will not march. But from now on we will not go to work.'

We wanted to see what was happening, so we drove by car to Nyanga West, where we saw a long line of men returning from Philippi police station. We passed on to Nyanga East, and found the same excitement. At Philippi we found thousands of men busy handing in their names. Later we went through to Cape Town to see some of our men who had been arrested. At the 'Contact' office, Mr Patrick Duncan was excited about the campaign. He said: 'You have poked the bees, but now you must be very careful. Anything can happen tonight.'

Back at Langa at 6 pm I heard a volley of shots. Another volley, then another, and the crackle of isolated shots. I felt a great sorrow and confusion. I ran towards the shooting. I met a woman who had been hit in the arm. Her hand was swollen and she wore no shoes. 'Police, my son, police . . . We were sitting quietly, and they fell on us with batons.' She walked away very fast. Again a volley rang out – koko, koko, koko, koko, thu-khu, thu-khu. And another volley. I felt that every bullet was felling a man. Ra-ta-ta-ta-ta-ta, thu-khu. I was panting with frightened anger. I cut through the fleeing crowd as the shooting stopped. 'How many have been killed? Sisi, how many are dead?'

'Only one, I think. The Saracens are firing high, but I saw one bleeding man being taken into Block B.'

People set the permit office and the general administration building on fire. At 9 pm we stopped the car and listened to the radio. We heard the news that over sixty had been killed at Sharpeville, and about 140 injured. On Sunday came the news that Chief Luthuli had burnt his pass and proclaimed 28 March as a day of mourning for Sharpeville and Langa. People were asked not to go to work that day. Then we learned that there was to be a nationwide round-up of African political leaders. Early on Wednesday morning Messrs Nxelewa, Makwetu, Shuba and others were arrested.

I went to the doctor that morning for medical treatment. Later someone called me to come and look at Washington Street. There was a long line of marching men. A child told me they were going to Caledon Square. Why? Nobody knew. I ran very fast to reach the head of the procession. An American reporter gave me a lift in his jeep, and we caught up just as the procession reached the Athlone-Pinelands railway line. The men told me they were on their way to protest because the police had assaulted some of them at Langa New Flats that morning. I suggested that our objective should be not the police, but the Minister of Justice, Mr Erasmus. They agreed and placed themselves under my leadership.

When we reached Mowbray station, many thousands who had been travelling by bus and train joined us in our march. At Groote Schuur we stopped to wait for stragglers, while I addressed the crowd. I told the men that without complete discipline, there would be chaos. I warned them to obey my commands implicitly. We marched on.

At Caledon Square, Colonel Terblanche was waiting. 'What's wrong now, Kgosana?' he asked. I told him the march had occurred spontaneously because the police had assaulted people in their homes, and that we insisted on meeting the Minister of Justice. Colonel Terblanche agreed to fix up the appointment, and asked me to come to Caledon Square at 5 pm to confirm the arrangement. In the meantime, he asked that the men return home peacefully. I gave the command, and the 30 000 demonstrators turned as one man and made their way home. Together with other leaders, I remained in town, waiting for the appointment. At 5.30 pm we entered Caledon Square. Captain Van Der Westhuizen was there to meet us. He said: 'The Minister is not interested in seeing you. A State of Emergency has been declared, and the country now operates under a new law altogether. You are all immediately under arrest.' □

Philip Kgosana

Back to exile

Ben Baartman got back to Worcester too late to bury his wife. Friends told him it had been a big funeral. But, alone in the graveyard, he paid his last respects to her.

During the last few days he had at home he tried to comfort his children, read them stories from the Bible.

Drum: March 1960 Big Ben Baartman came back to Worcester. By the grace of the South African government, which had banished him to a far-distant territory for reasons unstated, he was allowed back for two weeks to find a home for his children after his wife died while he was in exile. But they only gave him a fortnight. Then he had to leave his children without even a mother to console them.

In July 1959 the government banished Ben Baartman from his home in the Kwezi location to Ingwavuma, a remote part of Natal. Ben ran into a lot of misery at Ingwavuma. He was given a water-logged hut with snakes around it. He pressed for better conditions and thus antagonised a certain official who vowed he would 'break Ben Baartman's kaffir spirit'. Then came the news of the sudden death of his wife. Ben was heartbroken. The government granted him a fortnight to visit Worcester and arrange for the care of his children. Ben arrived too late for

ANC leader Ben Baartman banished from his family and home to a water-logged hut

Photographs by Halim's

his wife's funeral, but friends had taken photographs to show him that it had been a tremendous affair with hundreds of people.

For Ben the fortnight was a time for renewing friendships, making the most of the valuable hours with his four children, and for spending time in quiet meditation at the graveside of his wife near the location. 'The Nationalists' time will come. And I, for one, am prepared to wait for that time.' So saying, Ben left Worcester to return to Ingwavuma, leaving four children to live with his mother-in-law. □

'When an African is found to be responsible for disturbing the public order, he will be sent to some other Bantu area where the people have different affiliations and where he will consequently have little influence'
As stated by the Native Affairs Department

At the dark station, early in the morning, he said goodbye to his children. Then he had to leave.

Treason Trial resumes

In January 1960 the Treason Trial had started up again and lumbered into its fourth year.

Lunch hour with fellow defendants. Helen Joseph, member of the Executive Committee of the Federation of South African Women: 'People of all races can and will overcome the inhumanity of racism.'

Mandela, a keen amateur boxer, after sitting in the dock all day, went to Gerry Moloi's boxing gym every evening, often shadow-sparring with the champion Moloi himself, before working in his law office until late at night.

Chief Albert Luthuli, since banished, and Oliver Tambo. Both Luthuli and Tambo were discharged from the trial in 1958. Oliver Tambo, Deputy President-General, left South Africa in late 1959 to help launch the international economic boycott of South Africa.

Not one guilty in the Treason Trial

Photographs by Bob Gosani and Alf Kumalo

It cost nearly half a million pounds. It wasted four and a half years. It caused misery and suffering to hundreds among the accused and their families. Not one person was guilty. Nothing was achieved. It should never have happened!

Drum: July 1961 The most feared day in South Africa's saddest political trial had come. The accused, twenty-five men and two women, sat in neat rows and waited to hear about their fate. Their charge of high treason, for which the maximum penalty is death, had kept them on trial for more than four years. Jobs had been lost, families torn apart. What next?

The three judges, specially appointed by the Minister of Justice, filed into the courtroom to answer this crucial question. They did it swiftly, like a flash of lighting. 'Not Guilty' was the verdict. It was incredible for some of the accused, too sweet and somewhat unreal. 'I could not believe my ears until the judges rose to leave the court,' said trade unionist Leslie Masina afterwards.

Jubilant men and women in the African villages around Johannesburg burst into dance and song, winding up with the African national anthem, God Bless Africa (Nkosi Sikelele Afrika). Looking back at four years of the Treason Trial evoked anger, rejoicing, depression, and just plain amazement. This was clearly the most absurd and tragic trial in the country's legal history. Yet only those who saw the beginning of the Treason Trial could appreciate it in full.

Lunch break during the trial. The defendants in a church ground near the courtroom. The trial was heard in an old synagogue, which had been converted into a court. Left, Ahmed 'Kathy' Kathrada, Executive Member of the Indian Congress; F Ntshangani, leading Cape Congressite; J Nkadimeng, Johannesburg Trade Unionist; Sonia Bunting (drinking) and Nelson Mandela.

'I was immensely proud to be included in the frontline thirty, even though I did not know why I had been selected for this honour. I was proud to be sitting with them, sharing their ordeal with them' — Helen Joseph

It all started one day in December 1956. One hundred and fifty-six men and women of all races, but mostly Africans, were rounded up and arrested by the police. From various parts of the country, suspects were flown by military Dakotas or driven in police cars to Johannesburg for the preparatory examination into allegations of high treason.

The large Fort Hare Professor, Zacharias K Matthews, was sleeping in his own bed; three o'clock, just before dawn. Almost the next moment he was in a police car, speeding in the direction of a prison cell. 'High Treason', the charge was called. In Cape Town, Dr H M Moosa was waiting to see his sister-in-law get married, after flying specially from Johannesburg. Thirty minutes before the ceremony was to start, the police materialised. 'High Treason, Dr Moosa, High Treason!' In another few moments, the Doctor was on his way to the cells. In Johannesburg, nosey reporters called at the home of Mr and Mrs Slovo. 'Mummy has gone to jail,' said little girl Shawn. This was very high treason. From every section of the South African community, men and women were arrested.

Most of the suspects were drawn from the African National Congress, the South African Indian Congress, the South African Coloured Peoples' Organisation and the all-white Congress of Democrats. They had taken leading roles in the struggle against apartheid in the Union. Even before their preparatory examination began, the nation reacted with sharp placards: *We stand by our leaders!*

Came the first day of the preparatory examination at the Drill Hall, Johannesburg. Hundreds of people gathered outside the makeshift court to watch the 156 accused face the magistrate. 'Mayibuye! Afrika!' the crowd thundered. Next day the accused were put into a tall wire cage. Someone planted a notice on the cage: *Do not feed.* People laughed, and the notice came down. Meanwhile, the police clashed with the crowd outside, and heads were broken. A police detective from Kenya who had come to watch, received a baton-bashing on the head.

Those who thought this was a crazy trial did not know how much more drama was in store. A witness, Solomon Mgubasi, stepped into the witness box and described himself as a Bachelor of Arts, coming to give evidence against the accused. A witness, a police detective, Sergeant D Sogoni, told the court, reading from a speech made at a meeting by one of the women accused: 'A certain night,' the speech read, 'when Chief Luthuli was asleep, he heard a voice in his dream say, "Where are you, Luthuli?" and he answered, "Here I am, my Lord," and the voice said, "Go and lead my people out of the bondage of oppression".'

'How much nonsensical gibberish like this is going to be read into the record?' exploded Advocate Berrange at one stage. But the police were determined to build the largest, strongest case. Det-Sgt T Moeller brought in a book called *The Russian Recipes*, but could not remember why he had taken it during a search. 'Did you think this recipe book might have dealt with revolutionary tactics?' asked Advocate Slovo.

The crazy case lumbered on. It became boring and tedious. Some of the accused fell asleep. 'This is a court of law,' warned the magistrate. 'I hope that the people in the dock realise that this is a serious matter.' The accused sat up. But seriousness was not to be a permanent affair. It was shattered suddenly when a metal folding-seat collapsed with a crash under the weight of a police sergeant.

Soon after the preparatory examination, the Attorney-General sprang a surprise on the accused. More than fifty names were dropped from the indictment, including that of Albert Luthuli, former President-General of the now-banned African National Congress. Later on, more names were removed from the indictment (supposedly to be tried later), leaving only thirty.

That was the crazy side of the treason case. But there was the tragic end of it too. People lost their jobs. Public funds were sunk by the thousand into the case. The Treason Trial Defence Fund had to raise £100 000 as a temporary target to meet the costs of defence and subsistence allowances. Each of the accused who needed help were limited to £11 a month, from which they were to pay rent, clothe themselves and send children to school, among other things. An Afrikaans independent weekly newspaper reported 'on good authority' that pay for the head of the prosecution team, Mr Pirow, would be fixed at £25 000 for the duration of the case, then expected to last between four and six months. The fees for Mr Pirow's four juniors were estimated at between £16 000 and £17 000 each.

'We will continue our struggle,' say the acquitted

Photograph by Jurgen Schadeberg

But the Treason Trial brought sudden world attention to the South African situation, and it often provided an effective platform for the leaders. Det-Sgt Coetzee, for instance, read a speech by the famed women's leader, Mrs Ngoyi: 'We have thousands and thousands of coloureds with Afrikaner parents,' the record read. 'What's the good of apartheid in the streets, when there is not apartheid under the blanket?' Robert Resha, former executive member of the now banned ANC, was quoted as saying: 'When we speak of the people of South Africa, we speak of those people who have made South Africa their home. And when we say the people shall govern, we mean that Strijdom, Dr Dadoo, Chief Luthuli and Dr Van Der Ross will go to the polls together, and vote.'

Now the Treason Trial accused have been found not guilty and discharged, bringing a swift end to the country's craziest, most tragic case. The defence counsel were awarded a victory, even before they were through with stating their case. For the twenty-seven accused who formed the last batch to sit on trial in Pretoria, it's back to normal at last! □

Nathaniel Nakasa

On 13 October 1958, Moses Kotane, left, and Nelson Mandela beam out of the Court in seconds. For the moment there is nothing that can worry them. The Crown has withdrawn the indictment. A few months later, on 19 January 1959, Nelson Mandela and twenty-nine others were put on trial again.

Republic Day

United Front members lead a big march along London's Oxford Street at the time of the Prime Ministers' Conference. Second from left, Oliver Tambo, Kusen Guizi, Dr Yusuf Dadoo, Fenner Brockway, Labour MP, and Nana Mahomo. Dr Verwoerd had just arrived and delivered a 'No interference with our policies' speech.

In October 1960, the Verwoerd government held a referendum among the white population to proclaim the country a republic. The majority voted in favour. The date of the proclamation of the Republic was set for the fifty-first anniversary of the Union, 31 May 1961. At the Commonwealth Prime Ministers' Conference in London in March 1961, the majority of the Prime Ministers were against the continued membership of South Africa because of apartheid. On 15 March Verwoerd informed the Conference that he was withdrawing South Africa's application to remain a member of the Commonwealth after it became a Republic

Dr Verwoerd's Commonwealth walk-out was the United Front's biggest victory

Drum: April 1961 Dr Verwoerd's walk-out from the Commonwealth is a severe setback to the whole business and financial structure of the Union. Its political consequences must be tremendous, and will be felt increasingly, year after year. To one group it represents a signal victory – the South African politicians in exile known as the 'United Front'. On 8 March when Dr Verwoerd was shaking hands with Sir Abubakah Tafawa Balewa, it was five to one that South Africa would remain inside the Commonwealth. One week later, South Africa was out. How had it happened?

Those primarily responsible for the most severe defeat Dr Verwoerd has ever met in his whole political career, were a small group of exiles from South Africa itself. They include Dr Yusuf Dadoo, the Indian leader; Oliver Tambo, former Secretary of the ANC; Nana Mahomo, ex-PAC National Executive; Gaur Radebe, Tennyson Makiwane, Peter Molotsi and others.

How did they do it? The answer: by an intensive campaign of political lobbying. At the beginning of February a United Front delegation left London by air for India, Pakistan, Ceylon and Malaya. Their avowed purpose was to urge the Prime Ministers of these countries to stand firm at the Prime Ministers' Conference against South Africa being allowed to remain inside the Commonwealth. 'We believe,' said a spokesman, 'that only through the isolation of South Africa will it be possible to compel the government of Dr Verwoerd to change its policies, or to compel a change of government.' Besides personal visits to the Asian countries, a memorandum was sent at the same time to the premiers of Australia, New Zealand, Canada, Ghana and Nigeria.

Back after a successful tour, the United Front – which includes leaders of the banned ANC, the banned PAC, the SA Indian Congress and the Coloured People's Organisation – got to work organising marches and demonstrations in the United Kingdom, particularly in London. Finally, while the Conference was actually on, they exerted themselves to make contact with the different Commonwealth premiers and to put forward forcefully their point of view.□

Fourteen hundred delegates went to Maritzburg, where they sounded a new and powerful call for unity

Ex-ANC leader Nelson Mandela calls for a non-racial constitution in South Africa

Drum: May 1961 The odds were against success, and yet the outcome was a triumph, an indication of a new spirit. Few meetings can have been preceded by so many unfavourable omens as the All-In Africa Conference at Maritzburg.

There was the ban on the two main political organisations, the round-ups and imprisonment of leaders, the last-minute withdrawal of some Liberal Party and ex-PAC men, the difficulty of finding accommodation for delegates, the problems of transport. There was the decision to change the hall after tape-recording wires were reported to have been found in the original venue.

Yet despite all this, 1 400 delegates from all over the Union got to Pietermaritzburg. They came by train, by car, on foot, by bicycle. They came carrying bundles of food, which they shared as if on a family picnic. The picnic spirit at Maritzburg was all for the open spaces. Inside the hall the labourers, the clerks, peasants, ministers of religion, intellectuals, people from all walks of life, got down determinedly to discuss the need for united political action.

They talked, they listened, they argued, and at the end they crystallised their feelings in resolutions. They called for a 'non-racial, democratic constitution' in South Africa. They demanded the holding of a national convention of elected representatives of all adult men and women on an equal basis, irrespective of race, colour or creed. The convention should be called by the government not later than 31 May.

If the government ignored this demand, the conference resolved that country-wide demonstrations would be held on the eve of the intended proclamation of the Republic. The conference also called on the Indian and coloured communities, and all 'democratic Europeans' to join in opposing a regime 'which is bringing disaster to South Africa'.

Nelson Mandela made a strong plea for unity, which left its mark on all the talk that followed. 'We should emerge from this conference with the fullest preparations for a fully representative multi-racial national convention. From this conference will come the foundation of a fully democratic government,' he told the gathering. Mr Mandela paid tribute to the role played last year by the banned African organisations. The ANC, which for nearly fifty years had been 'the sword and shield of the African people', had been suppressed. The people, he said, were now faced with two alternatives. They had either to accept discrimination, humiliation, Pondolands, the betrayal of the true interests of the African people, appeasement. That was one choice. The alternative was to stand firm for their rights.

The people could allow themselves to remain disunited in the face of the government's arrogance, or they could stand united to ensure that the government's discriminatory legislation did not work. The way had already been shown by the United Front, whose efforts had resulted in South Africa resigning from the Commonwealth. This type of unity was possible here too. □

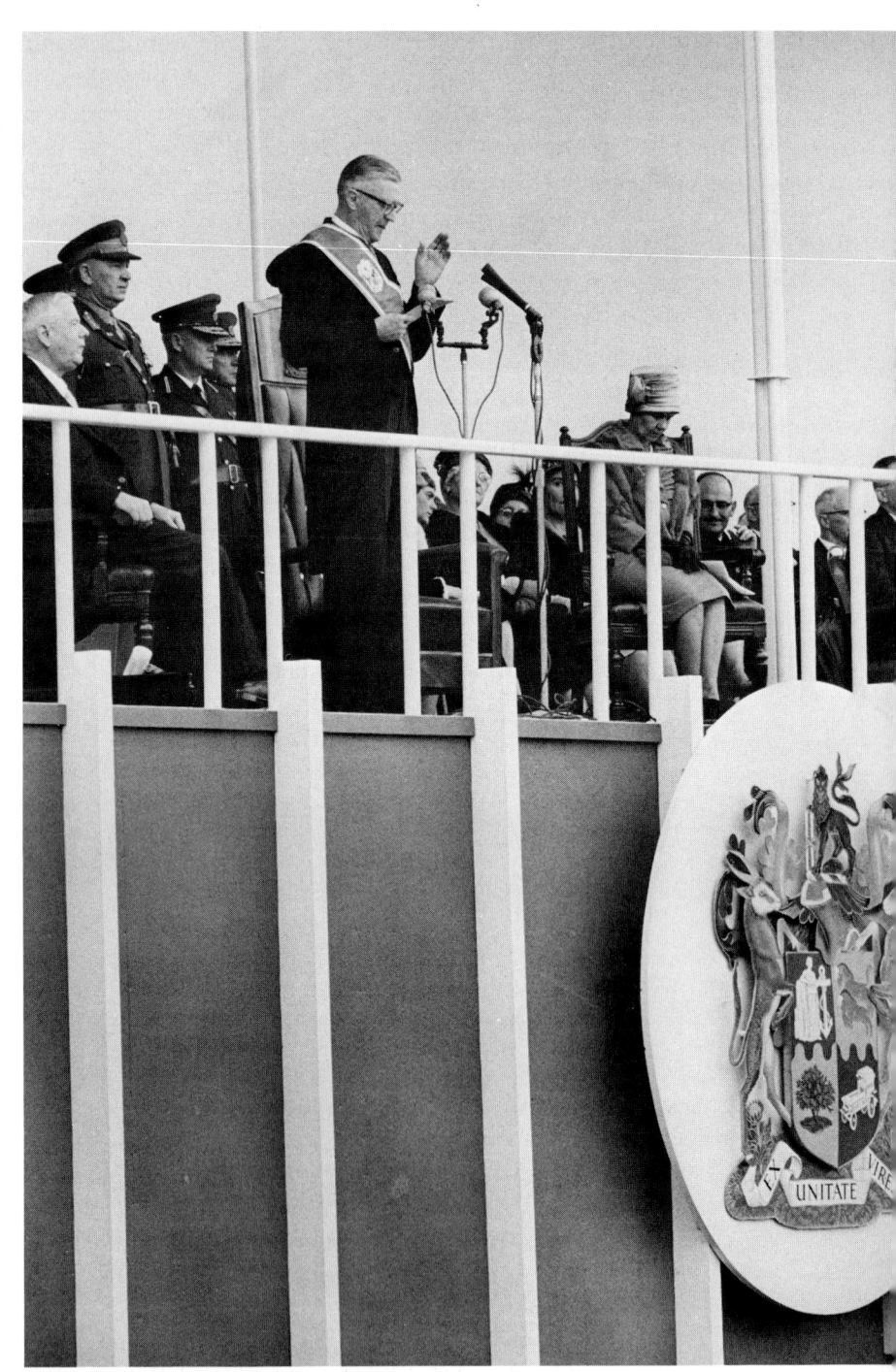

31 May 1961. It rained heavily and continuously as C R Swart, the former Minister of Justice, was sworn in as the first President of the Republic of South Africa in Church Square, Pretoria.

The days of crisis from the Maritzburg Conference of March until 29, 30 and 31 May, the days of the stay-at-home and the Republic celebrations

Drum: July 1961 Round 1 of the 1961 'test of nerves' between the Congress alliance and the government is over – and the government claims a victory. The avowed aim of the National Action Council was to get the Prime Minister to call a national convention to decide on a new multi-racial constitution and, failing that, to demonstrate non-violently against a Republic brought into being without the consultation or consent of the non-white people by a nationwide, three-day stay-at-home.

The plan behind it was to:
1. demonstrate to the non-white people and white opponents of apartheid their own solidarity and strength;
2. test the effectiveness of their economic weapon: the withdrawal of labour; and
3. ensure that celebrations of Republic Day would be held in an atmosphere of tension as a result of the non-violent 'demonstration'.

This was not a secret plan. Nelson Mandela and the other leaders had never made any attempt to conceal it. But it just didn't come off. Before the event, plans for the stay-at-home had caused such concern that the Army was mobilised; meetings were banned; the police conducted special day and night patrols; thousands of Africans were arrested; white women joined pistol clubs; and there was widespread hoarding of food.

But between breakfast and lunch on Monday, 29 May, the government, the daily press, and the white public had written off the stay-at-home as a failure. By Tuesday, 30 May, they had forgotten that any threat ever existed. And so Republic Day, 31 May, was celebrated in triumph. It was the Day of the Afrikaner, with nothing to spoil it – except the rain. Some of the people who stayed up all night on the pavements of Pretoria in the wet and cold began their working days in the Republic of South Africa with coughs and sniffles. But they had their Day.

For millions of our non-white people it was just another day which had nothing to do with them. A few Chiefs, coloureds, Indians and one Malay had seats at the ceremony in Pretoria – and had their pictures in the papers and on the newsreels. There was free meat and beer in the locations around Pretoria for those who wanted it. At Goodwood showgrounds in Cape Town there were fewer than 50 coloureds and Africans among the 6 000 crowd of mainly Afrikaners. In Cape Town it was estimated that only one in ten coloured children had accepted the Republican medal. In the Transvaal some Indian children threw away the flags but kept the sticks. In Durban Mr E G Rooks, President of the Coloured Federal Council, said 'The majority of coloured people did not allow their children to accept medals and flags because of their grievances and the many hardships that the legislators have caused them.

'But we are now citizens of a Republic of South Africa and for our part we shall strive to be loyal to the Republic and remain law-abiding as we have been in the past. It is to be hoped that the government will be able to afford a more magnanimous attitude now that the nearest and dearest wish of their hearts has been fulfilled. Just as they have always yearned for a free motherland, so we too, with all our countrymen yearn for the day when we will be first-class citizens and live happily in the Republic of South Africa.'

The general picture emerging from what happened at the end of May is that more than half our non-white people in South Africa wanted to go about their daily lives quietly and uninvolved. But tens of thousands – more than one in three workers in the main cities and towns – did respond to the call to stay at home.

According to Mr Nelson Mandela there was a more than 60 per cent stay-away in Johannesburg, about 75 per cent in Port Elizabeth (on the second day), between 50 and 60 per cent in Durban and about 50 per cent among the coloureds in the Cape. In Middelburg in the Transvaal all businesses came to a complete standstill. Indian shops and factories closed in almost all the main centres and in scores of small towns and rural dorps. These were the days of confusion. But there was also a fair degree of discipline. The leaders had emphasised to their followers: 'No violence!' and, with the exception of Port Elizabeth, there were no major incidents. There were some assaults in the townships, but no more than the 'normal' quota of everyday life. The Dutch Reformed Church at Evaton was set alight and damaged, but that was on the Saturday night.

The people didn't lose their sense of humour. 'So you're a Republican now. I see you've stayed away from work in honour of the Republic.'

The shebeen queens did a brisk trade, except those who make their money from miners. The mines had tightened up security measures by refusing permits to leave the mines, and allowing no visitors. One shebeen queen told *Drum* reporter Duke Ngcobo: 'I normally sell seven tins of hops a day to the boys at the mines. But since

Verwoerd versus Mandela

Almost immediately after becoming a member of the Senate in 1948, Dr Verwoerd spelled out in a speech the government's apartheid policy, here under the heading 'Natives in towns'.

'The Party appreciates the danger of the influx of natives into the towns and undertakes to preserve the European character of our towns, and to take energetic and effective measures for the safety of persons as well as of property and for the peaceful life of urban residents.

'All natives must be placed in separate residential areas, and their concentration in our urban areas must be counteracted. The native in our urban areas must be regarded as a "visitor", who will never have the right to claim any political rights or equal social rights with the Europeans in the European area.'

'What had happened in London was not a defeat but a victory . . . We have freed ourselves from the Afro-Asian states,' Verwoerd said after his return from the Commonwealth Prime Ministers' Conference. 'So many nations have had to get their complete freedom by armed struggle . . . but here we have reached something which we never expected.'

a week ago my business has been down to one tin a day.' A call-girl said: 'I wish I could catch hold of this Mandela and make him pay for all I have lost.'

The National Action Council had two full months in which to prepare for the stay-at-home. Its members worked day and night for the success of the plan. Its secretary, Nelson Mandela, emerged as a dynamic personality with a high sense of the dramatic. Mandela – forced to work behind the scenes for ten years under two five-year banning orders – burst onto the scene at Maritzburg only ten days after his banning order had expired.

Mandela soon proved to be the best public relations officer the Congress movement had ever known. When the police swooped, Mandela and his fellow leaders went into hiding. The security men, who had said they would 'skim the cream off non-white leadership as it rises' started a man-hunt for Mandela and his colleagues. It went on for a month, but scarcely a day passed without Mandela making the headlines.

There were telephone calls to the newspaper editors – Mandela's became one of the best-known voices in South Africa – and secret meetings with newspapermen. In disguise and out of disguise, Nelson Mandela was very much at large – under the noses of the police – making statements, making plans. With Mandela exuding confidence and emphasising non-violence, and government spokesmen putting up a barrage of counter-propaganda, no African political campaign has ever had such nation-wide publicity. The National Action Council was divided into twenty-five areas, each with a full-time organiser, part-time sub-organisers and 'activists'. All this made a big impact on the more politically minded section of the non-white population, and for the first time it extended to the coloureds too. But the stay-at-home call did not succeed in

The biggest surprise was the power exerted by the Pan African Congress

Photographs by Alf Kumalo

'Unless responsible leadership is given to canalise and control the feelings of our people, there will be outbreaks of terrorism which will produce an intensity of bitterness and hostility between the various races of this country . . .' Nelson Mandela

Drum has taken its own survey of the stay-at-home campaign. Here is a statement by the campaign leader, Mr Nelson Mandela.

Mr Mandela says: 'The response to the stay-at-home call of the All-In African National Council was solid and substantial and a great deal more successful than was made out at the time of the strike in order to smother it at birth. Few organisations in the world could have withstood and survived the full-scale and massive bombardment directed against us by the government during the last month.

'It has been said that appeals for action should concentrate on bread-and-butter issues. Of course the African people are moved by bread-and-butter issues. Who isn't? We demand higher wages, lower rents. But Africans need the vote to legislate decent laws. This is the importance of the demand for a new National Convention. One-man-one-vote is the key to our future.'

Will the stay-at-home type of campaign be abandoned? 'The African people will understand that there is no sense in announcing our next tactics now. Let us just say that new ways will always be found. As for myself, I have made my decision. I am not quitting South Africa. This is my country and my homeland. The freedom movement is my life, and I shall strive side by side with the brave sons and daughters of Africa until the end of my days.'

fully capturing the imagination of many non-politically minded people.

They were confused by a press report of 'secret plans' to hold demonstrations in the cities (which Mandela indignantly repudiated). They were confused by the shower of leaflets from PAC, from 'African Nationalists', from the 'Sons of Zululand', telling them to ignore the call to stay at home because this was a white man's issue. And they were influenced by warnings from government departments, from chiefs of industry and commerce and other employers telling them that if they failed to report for work, they would either be dismissed or lose pay. They saw the Saracens and the troop-carriers, they were told that a strike was illegal, and they didn't want trouble.

PAC supporters – or African Nationalists as they now call themselves – are saying: 'We told you so'. They say they had warned the people that it was 'the wrong kind of campaign' and that it would collapse. In a statement to *Drum*, Mr Z B Molefe, a leader of the 'African Nationalists' described the call for a national convention and the stay-at-home as a 'back-door campaign'. He said the nature of the campaign was confused between talk of demonstrations, protests, stay-at-home and general strike; that the African people had no interest in the Republican issue; and that 'the real organisers disappeared. They relied on conducting the campaign from public phone boxes, with the result that the people were left leaderless.'

The African National Congress has bitterly criticised the part played by the PAC in obstructing the stay-at-home. ☐

The last days of Cato Manor

> **Group Areas 'axe' hits 40 000 Indians in Cato Manor**
>
> *January 1963* The final blow of the Group Areas axe has now fallen on the homes of nearly 40 000 Indian residents of Cato Manor. In a letter to the co-ordinating Council, Mr P W Botha, Minister of Community Development and Housing, says he is not prepared to repeal the proclamation of 1958. The proclamation, which made Cato Manor 'white', means that the residents will have to move soon.
>
> The Group Areas decision means that a settled community will have to lose millions of rand in property value. They will have to break down their temples, their mosques and churches and even their schools. The land involved will amount to hundreds of acres. They will even have to leave behind their cemetery where they have buried their dead for nearly a century. Mr Botha's letter says: 'Ample opportunity is made available for the Indian community in Natal to develop its own area.'

Drum: November 1963 The Saracen screams its way up the steep hill like a giant. All around are squalid shacks. Pot-bellied children stand watching. Women with yesterday's meal still on their dresses mutter to themselves. Soon a convoy of police vehicles goes up the hill. Shrill voices shout: 'Mileko! Mileko!' Stony-eyed policemen peer into the gathering twilight and see the forms of little children running amid the shacks.

As the evening gathers, there is a strange quiet about the shack-town. Policemen are gathered at the beerhall, waiting for signs of trouble. Suddenly the quietness is broken by the 'kikizaing' of women. Men and women pour down the hillsides onto the market square. Soon the administration buildings are alight. Looters take what they can lay their hands on before flames destroy what is left of the building. Powerful searchlights mounted on a hilltop streak through the darkness. Then peace comes again over the township. It's late in the night and the township sullenly goes to sleep.

It's Sunday morning. And it's drinking day. This is the one day that most men in the area look forward to. They drink every mixture that is available to drown their miseries. Fat, huge-breasted women stir the brew buried in forty-four gallon drums in the ground to feed the thirst of the never-ending stream of customers. There are fights and there are killings. All through the day there is laughter and gaiety in the township. Children run in the open spaces, ragged and dirty. Some, in their Sunday best, head for church.

It's Monday morning. Long before the sun has risen, already thousands of people stand in long, winding queues to wait for the buses to take them to work. Cato Manor is ready to begin another week – another week that will see more of the tragedy, more of the fun, more of the bustling life that made it South Africa's craziest township.

This was Cato Manor, the most repulsive and yet the most romantic slum in Natal. It housed almost 125 000 people and was in the spotlight of the world press for many a year. Today, Cato Manor has virtually disappeared. Only a small portion of it remains to be cleared and only a handful of people are still waiting to be taken to the newly developed townships to the north and south of Durban.

I have seen Cato Manor in all its moods – anger, sorrow, gaiety, remorse, lawlessness – over the past ten years. Recently I drove through the once-sprawling township. The change in the area was stark and vivid. The famous market-place of Cato Manor has disappeared. In its place is lush undergrowth. Further up the street, once-busy shops are either broken down or barred. As I drove up the hill towards the 'kwa-ticky' area – where nine policemen were butchered a few years ago – I saw clearings all around me where shacks once stood. On the one hillside where the shacks still remained, there was a strange sobriety. A small police car drove through the road ahead of me. There were no longer the taunting cries of the shack people. Two men were breaking down their shacks. An old man put together a few pieces of iron and cardboard. This was his new home until he was moved out of the area. Lower down the hillside, a cow stood framed in the window of what was once a shop. Little urchins were darting in and out of the wreck playing with the cow. On the wall of the building still stood a sign 'Asisebenzi May 29, 30, 31. Stay at Home' – a reminder of the political hey-days of Cato Manor. On the main street leading to Durban stood the remains of the administration building framed by a large tree. Like almost all of the one-time business centres, it stood in ruins.

This then, is Cato Manor, 1963. This is what is left of what only a couple of years ago was a pulsating township. This is the ghost of Cato Manor. □

G R Naidoo

In 1958 Cato Manor was officially proclaimed white. 125 000 people – Indians, Africans and a few thousand whites – lived in the 4 500 acres of Cato Manor. Most of the land was owned by Indians, let out to African tenants who divided up their plots, letting portions to sub-tenants

Photographs by G R Naidoo

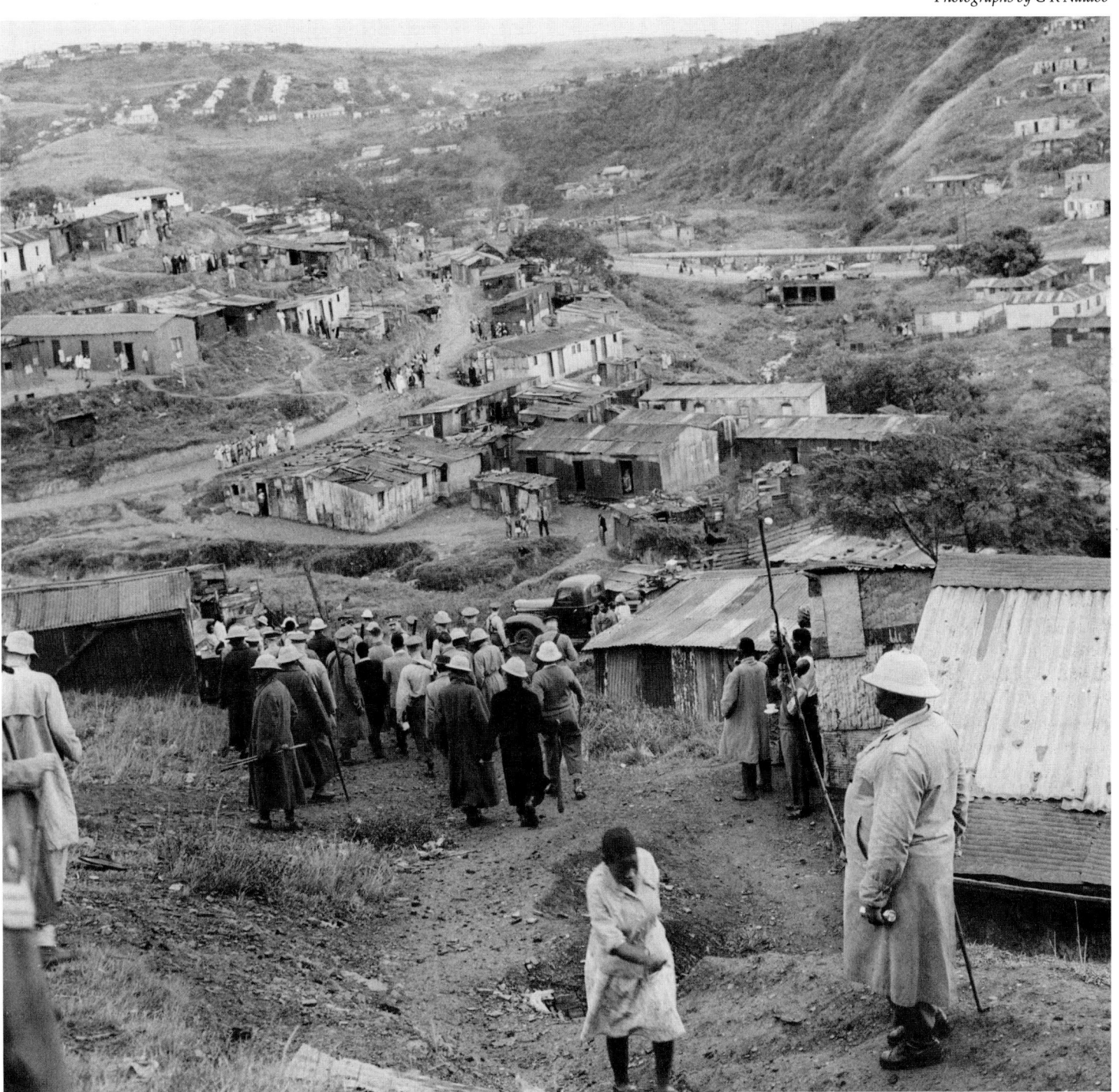

Today the once-bustling Cato Manor is almost a ghost town. Once the street thronged with life. Now many of the houses have disappeared and only a handful of people remain.

The Rivonia sabotage trial

The raid

Drum: August 1963 Thursday night, 11 July 1963. A bakery van and a dry cleaner's van trundle down the long driveway of an elegant house in Rivonia, a smart northern suburb of Johannesburg. From the vans come police. They fan out and surround the house and outbuildings. With them are two highly trained police dogs. A police officer enters a biggish room in an outbuilding, and sixteen people tense in surprise.

One, Mr Walter Sisulu, ANC Secretary-General, whom the police have been hunting for several months, leaps to a window. But on the outside a snarling police dog forces him back. Another man makes a break for it, but a dog brings him down. Then they realise that it's the end. Handcuffs are snapped on and all but one do not resist. The man who declines the proferred handcuffs is Mr Ahmed 'Kathy' Kathrada, popular former Indian congressman whom the police have also sought since he skipped his house-arrest order a few months back. The handcuffs are forced onto his wrists.

And, as detectives fan out into the house and spread over the 22-acre grounds, the arrested people are rounded up and taken off to 90-day detention. They include Mr Govan Mbeki of Port Elizabeth; Mr Lionel Bernstein, a twelve-hour arrestee; Dennis Goldberg, former member of the Congress of Democrats, and Mr B A Hepple, a Johannesburg advocate. With them go well-known South African artist Arthur Goldreich, his wife, Hazel, and Dr Hilliard Festenstein. Mr Goldreich had driven into the grounds of the house soon after the swoop. When he realised something was amiss, he tried to reverse his car back to the road, but police clambered onto the bonnet of the vehicle and he was forced to stop at the point of a revolver. Mrs Goldreich was arrested too, as she drove into the grounds. Dr Festenstein, a medical researcher, has been held in similar circumstances.

After the raid, police announce that they have unearthed many documents, a radio transmitter and other evidence. And, they say, they have broken the back of the ANC underground and the 'Umkhonto we Sizwe' movement. No journalists were there when the raid took place, and nobody was allowed near the house. □

South Africa goes on trial

Drum: December 1963 All South Africa is on trial: its political leaders, its people, its government. For the men now charged at the country's three major sabotage trials are not alone in their predicament. The very people who introduced the legislation under which the men are being charged, are themselves on trial – on trial before the world.

At the United Nations, at meetings of international jurists and at special gatherings in many countries, the South African government has been condemned both for its Sabotage Act and for putting these men on trial. There are scores of sabotage trials throughout the country, but the world's attention is focused on the three major hearings and, in particular, on the Pretoria trial which arose out of the spectacular Rivonia raid. Not since the Treason Trial has there been so much world interest in South African judicial proceedings. The three trials are completely separate and the charges against the men in each one are different. Whatever the outcome, *Drum* says that it is a tragedy that outstanding and brilliant men like Nelson Mandela, Walter Sisulu, Billy Nair and Neville Alexander should be standing trial today instead of being able to play active – and vital – roles in running the country.

The whole world was watching when the three major sabotage trials started in Pretoria, Cape Town and Pietermaritzburg. The people charged in the three places are:

- Pretoria: Nelson Mandela, Walter Sisulu, Dennis Goldberg, Lionel 'Rusty' Bernstein, Govan Mbeki, Ahmed 'Kathy' Kathrada, James Kantor, Andrew Mlangeni, Elias Motsoaledi and Raymond Mahlaba.
- Cape Town: Neville Alexander, Don Davis, Marcus Solomons, Elizabeth van den Heyden, Fikili Bam, Ian Leslie van den Heyden, Lionel Davis, Dorothy Alexander, Dulcie September, Doris van den Heyden and Gordon Hendricks.
- Maritzburg: Ebrahim Ismail, Girja Singh, Natvarial Babenia, Billy Nair, Kisten Moonsamy, George Naicker, Kisten Doorsamy, Curnick Ndhlovu, Ragoowan Kistensamy, Riot Mkwanazi, Alfred Duma, Msizeni Shadrack Mapumulo, Mfanyane Bernard Nkosi, Zakela Mdhlalose, Matthews Meyiwa, Joshua Tembinkosi Zulu, Mdingeni David Mkize, David Ndawonde and Siva Pillay.

Nelson Mandela – The Black Pimpernel

In 1961 Nelson Mandela had finally realised that the passive resistance and non-violence movements had no effect on the government and that heavy petitions and protests addressed to the white authorities were ignored.

He and the other ANC leaders turned to a policy of violence against what they claimed was a violent regime.

The Rivonia raid of 11 July 1963 was followed by a trial in Pretoria, for which Nelson Mandela was brought out of prison to become accused number one

The first phase would be sabotage aimed at railway lines, power pylons, vacant installations and government buildings. If this had no effect guerilla warfare directed against military bases and police stations would begin. If this too did not persuade the whites to compromise and negotiate, complete armed struggle would be the only alternative.

Mandela, Sisulu and other ANC leaders and Communist Party members formed 'Umkhonto we Sizwe' (Spear of the Nation) to carry out the programme of graduated violence. In late 1961, in various parts of the country, cells were established and bombs exploded at symbolic targets.

As acts of sabotage continued, Mandela appeared and disappeared in many corners of South Africa, with the police being unable to catch him. For his elusiveness he became known as 'The Black Pimpernel'. In January 1962 Mandela was smuggled across the border and flown to Ethiopia where he met Oliver Tambo, who had been sent abroad to establish an external ANC presence. In Addis Ababa, Mandela addressed a conference of the Pan African Freedom Movement. Then he was in Algiers, where he met liberation leader Ben Bella. Later he appeared in London, where he met Hugh Gaitskell, then leader of the Labour Party, and Joe Grimond, then Liberal Party leader, seeking aid, arms and money from them.

On 5 August Nelson Mandela was arrested near Howick in Natal, posing as a chauffeur. He had been to a meeting with Chief Albert Luthuli, reporting back on his world trip. Mandela was tried in the Johannesburg regional court for leaving the country without a passport and for incitement to strike. He was sentenced to five years' imprisonment and sent to Robben Island, the maximum security prison for political prisoners, off-shore, within sight of Cape Town, where he was placed in solitary confinement.

By June 1963, more than 200 acts of sabotage had been committed in South Africa by 'The Spear of the Nation'. □

Drum: 1963 World-wide reactions to Rivonia continued this week, with arguments in the United Nations, a debate in the British House of Commons, comment in South Africa's House of Assembly, and continued discussion in the world press.

Meanwhile, Goldreich, Wolpe and two Indian detainees Moosa Mollan and A Jassat, bribed a guard at the Johannesburg Police Headquarters cells and escaped on 11 August. Goldreich and Wolpe, disguised as priests, made their way to Tanzania. To Security Branch police-

Winnie Mandela had to get special permission to attend the Rivonia Trial in Pretoria since she was restricted to Johannesburg district by a banning order. After permission was refused, Winnie made a personal appeal to the Prime Minister. He relented, but with a threat: 'Permission will be withdrawn at any time if your presence or action at the court, the manner in which you dress or in any other respect, lead to an incident caused by you or others present.'

men, Goldreich's escape was a disaster and they have little doubt that he too would have been sentenced to life imprisonment had he stood trial.

The accused face two charges of sabotage involving 192 counts, one of contravening the Suppression of Communism Act and one of contravening the Criminal Law Amendment Act. The State alleges that they, together with others named in the indictment as co-conspirators, planned the overthrow of the government by revolution and by assisting an armed invasion of South Africa by foreign troops.

Unless the government was prepared to settle its differences with the non-whites, a long, violent struggle lay ahead and the whites would have to pack their bags and go, said Lionel Bernstein at the Rivonia trial yesterday.

Bernstein, an architect, told the Judge-President, Mr Justice De Wet, that he was a Marxist and had been active in political affairs most of his adult life. Most of his political work had been confined to writings of a leftist nature. He had been an accused in the Treason Trial and had been banned three times.

Listen, White Man and *Spear of the Nation* were the titles of two pamphlets which were distributed in Port Elizabeth in 1963 in the name of the African National Congress, Detective-Sergeant P J du Preez told Mr Justice De Wet at the Rivonia trial yesterday.

Sisulu said the ANC pamphlet which said that the whites in South Africa would be 'faced with a war' was not a threat. Unless whites changed their attitudes they would be faced with a war. He added: 'It is inevitable that in any civil war fought in this country victory will go to the oppressed.' He said that the leaders of the National Liberation Movement were responsible people. The fact that men like Arthur Goldreich, Harold Wolpe and Jack Hodgson had left the country did not make them any less responsible. □

'Operation Mayibuye' – 'Operation Comeback'

Pretoria: 10 February 1964 At the Rivonia Sabotage Trial today the State handed in a document alleged to be the master-plan for the violent overthrow of the government. The prosecutor, Dr Percy Yutar, said the document had been found at Rivonia: 'It's the corner-stone of the whole case'. The document gave details of how military groups were to be landed at pre-selected areas and how they would be supported by guerilla forces.

'The white State has thrown overboard every pretence of rule by democratic process. Armed to the teeth, it has

Vorster: *The man responsible for guiding the Sabotage Act through Parliament, Balthazar John Vorster, South Africa's Minister of Justice. In a few years, he has risen from relative obscurity to eclipse Dr Verwoerd in the world's headlines. Before joining the Nationalist Party only eleven years ago, he was an Ossewabrandwag die-hard. Ironically, when the Nationalists swept to power in the 1948 election, he was beaten in the Brakpan constituency by a man who is now his Cabinet colleague, Mr A E Trollip, Minister of Labour, then a staunch United Party supporter.*

Mandela: *Like Vorster before his rise to fame, Nelson Mandela practised as a lawyer in Johannesburg. Other similarities: both have been detained for their political beliefs, Vorster during the war and Mandela several times in the last few years. Both are strong, forceful characters and both are highly respected by their followers. Mandela became known as the 'Black Pimpernel' when he went underground after the 1961 strike and for months evaded arrest. After he was picked up in Natal last year, he was found guilty of incitement and jailed for five years.*

Flyer issued by the command of 'Umkhonto we Sizwe' 16 December 1961.

Units of the 'Umkhonto we Sizwe' today carried out planned attacks against government installations, particularly those connected with the policy of apartheid and race discrimination.

'Umkhonto we Sizwe' will be at the front line of the people's defence. It will be the fighting arm of the people against the government and its policies of race oppression. It will be the striking force of the people for liberty, for rights and for their final liberation!

We of 'Umkhonto we Sizwe' have always sought to achieve liberation without bloodshed and civil clash. We hope that our first actions will awaken everyone to a realisation of the disastrous situation to which the Nationalist policy is leading. We hope that we will bring the government and its supporters to their senses before it is too late.

In these actions, we are working in the best interests of all the people of this country – black, brown and white – whose future happiness and well-being cannot be attained without the overthrow of the Nationalist government, the abolition of white supremacy and the winning of liberty, democracy and full national rights and equality for all people of this country.

---

presented the people with only one choice, and that is its overthrow by force and violence. Our target is that on arrival the external force should find at least 7 000 men in the four main areas ready to join the guerilla army in the initial onslaught.'

Main points of the plan are:
- To land four groups of thirty based on present resources either by ship or by air.
- To split the groups into platoons of ten.
- To supply arms to the local population.
- To take the enemy by surprise.
- To establish base areas.
- To set up a political authority which will in due course develop into a provisional revolutionary government.

Propaganda should be broadcast over the radio, leaflets should be dropped by air and trainees should be flown in regularly. Several committees should be set up to deal with intelligence, external planning, transport and logistics.

'I have cherished the ideal of a democratic and free society in which all persons live together in harmony and with equal opportunities. It is an ideal which I hope to live for, and to see realised. But my Lord, if needs be, it is an ideal for which I am prepared to die.' Nelson Mandela

Statement from the dock by Nelson Mandela, accused number one

'My Lord, I hold a Bachelor's degree in Arts and practised as an attorney in partnership with Mr Oliver Tambo. I am a convicted prisoner, serving five years for leaving the country without a permit, and for inciting people to go on strike at the end of May 1961.

'I admit immediately that I was one of the persons who helped to form "Umkhonto we Sizwe", and that I played a prominent role in its affairs until I was arrested in August 1962.

'In my youth in the Transkei, I listened to the elders of my tribe telling stories of the old days. Amongst the tales they related to me were those of wars fought by our ancestors in defence of the fatherland. The names of Dingane and Bambata, Hintsa and Makana, Squngathi and Dalasile, Moshoeshoe and Sekhukune were praised as the pride and glory of the entire African nation. I hoped then that life might offer me the opportunity to serve my people and make my own humble contribution to their freedom struggle. This is what has motivated me in all that I have done in relation to the charges made against me in this case.

'I do not deny that I planned sabotage. I planned it as a result of a calm and sober assessment of the political situation that had arisen after many years of tyranny, exploitation and oppression of my people by the whites. We believed that as a result of government policy, violence by the African people had become inevitable, and that unless responsible leadership was given to catalyse and control the feelings of our people, there would be outbreaks of terrorism which would produce an intensity of bitterness and hostility between the various races of this country which is not produced even by war.

'We felt that without sabotage there would be no way open to the African people to succeed in their struggle against the principle of white supremacy. All lawful modes of expressing opposition to this principle had been closed by legislation and we were placed in a position in which we had either to accept a permanent state of inferiority, or defy the government. We first broke the law in a way which avoided any recourse to violence, and when the government resorted to a show of force to crush opposition to its policies, only then did we decide to answer violence with violence. The violence which we chose to adopt was not terrorism. We who formed "Umkhonto" were all members of the ANC and had behind us the ANC tradition of non-violence. We believed that South Africa belonged to all the people who lived in it, and not to one group, be it black or white.

'In 1960 there was the shooting at Sharpeville which resulted in the declaration of the ANC as an unlawful organisation. We believed in the words of the Universal Declaration of Human Rights, that "the will of the people shall be the basis of the authority of the government", and for us to accept the banning was equivalent to accepting the silencing of Africans for all time. The ANC refused to dissolve, but instead went underground. We believed it was our duty to preserve this organisation which had been built up with almost fifty years of unremitting toil. What were we, the leaders of our people to do? Were we to give in to the show of force and the implied threat against future action, or were we to fight it out, and if so, how?

'How to continue to fight? We of the ANC had always stood for a non-racial democracy, and we shrank from any action which might drive the races further apart than they already were. But the hard facts were that fifty years of non-violence had brought the African people nothing but more and more repressive legislation, and fewer and fewer rights. When some of us discussed this in June 1961, it could not be denied that our policy to achieve a non-racial state by non-violence had achieved nothing, and that our followers were beginning to lose confidence in this policy, and were developing disturbing ideas of terrorism.

'It must not be forgotten that violence had, in fact, become a feature of the South African political scene. There had been violence in 1957, when the women of Zeerust were ordered to carry passes; there was violence in 1958, with the enforcement of Bantu Authorities and cattle culling in Sekhukhuneland; there was violence in 1959, when the people of Cato Manor protested against pass raids; there was violence in 1960, when the government attempted to impose Bantu Authorities in Pondoland. Thirty-nine Africans died in those Pondoland disturbances. In 1961 there had been riots in Warmbaths, and all this time, my Lord, the Transkei had been a seething mass of unrest.

'Each disturbance pointed clearly to the inevitable growth amongst Africans of the belief that violence was the only way out. It showed that a government which uses force to maintain its rule teaches the oppressed to use force to oppose it. At the beginning of June 1961, after a long and anxious assessment of the South African situation, I and some colleagues came to the conclusion that as violence in this country was inevitable, it would be unreal-

The historic Rivonia trial has ended and eight men have started serving life sentences imposed on them by Mr Justice Quartus de Wet in Pretoria last week

istic and wrong for African leaders to continue preaching peace and non-violence at a time when the government met our peaceful demands with force.

'It is true that there has often been close co-operation between the ANC and the Communist Party. But co-operation is merely proof of a common goal – in this case the removal of white supremacy – and is not proof of a complete community of interests. Perhaps the most striking illustration is to be found in the co-operation between Great Britain, the United States and the Soviet Union in the fight against Hitler. Nobody but Hitler would have dared suggest that such co-operation turned Churchill or Roosevelt into communists or communist tools, or that Britain and America were working to bring about a communist world. Even General Chiang Kai Shek, today one of the bitterest enemies of communism, fought together with the communists against the ruling classes.

'"Umkhonto" was formed by Africans to further their struggle for freedom in their own land. Communists and others supported the movement, and we only wish that more sections of the community would join us. Our fight is against real, and not imaginary hardships, or to use the language of the State Prosecutor, "so-called hardships". Basically, my Lord, we fight against two features which are the hallmark of African life in South Africa, and which are entrenched by legislation which we seek to have repealed. These features are poverty and lack of dignity, and we do not need communists, or so-called "agitators" to teach us about these things.'

Guilty as charged!

The offences of which the Rivonia trialists were guilty were essentially treasonous, but the State had not charged them with treason and he would not impose the death penalty, the Judge-President, Mr Justice De Wet, said yesterday when he sentenced the remaining accused to life imprisonment.

- Lionel Bernstein was acquitted and discharged, but was immediately rearrested after the court rose. He was taken down to the cells.
- Mandela was found guilty on all four counts.
- Sisulu was found guilty on all four counts.
- Goldberg was found guilty on all four counts.
- Mbeki was found guilty on all four counts.
- Kathrada was found guilty on the second count of sabotage only. Acquitted on counts one, three and four.
- Mhlaba was found guilty on all four counts.

Nelson Mandela and Walter Sisulu on Robben Island.

- Motsoaledi was found guilty on all four counts.
- Mlangesi was found guilty on all four counts.

'Sentence will be pronounced tomorrow', the Judge said.

Mrs Hilda Bernstein saw her husband shortly after his arrest. She said afterwards that he was arrested on a charge of breaking his banning orders on 11 July 1963, the day he was arrested at Rivonia.

The verdict was heard in absolute silence by the large crowd, among whom was Mrs Albertina Sisulu, dressed in tribal costume. The jury box was filled with observers, including the diplomatic representatives of Britain, the United States of America, the Netherlands and Japan.

The number of the accused was originally eleven, but after the charge against him had been withdrawn, Alexander Bob Hepple, a Johannesburg advocate, fled the country. The charge against James Kantor, a Johannesburg attorney, was dropped at the end of the State's case. Mr Kantor is now in Britain. □

If I were Prime Minister

When told he had won the Nobel Peace Prize, valued at more than £15 000, Chief Luthuli's first thought was not of the money, but of the honour. And he felt it to be an honour, not for himself alone, but for all the people of South Africa. Now Albert Luthuli tells Drum *what he would do if he were in power*

Drum: December 1961 The solution to the South African problem will call for radical reforms. The basic political need is for a government which is truly a government of all the people, for the people, and by the people. This can only be so in a state where all adults – regardless of race, colour or belief – are voters.

The whites, being a quarter of the population, possess 87 per cent of the country's land in freehold. Africans, who form three-quarters of the population, were allocated by legislation only 13 per cent of the land, some of it poor land. Of this land, 99 per cent is trust land; only about one per cent or less is held by Africans in freehold. In trust land, Africans are virtually state tenants.

To meet this man-made inequality will demand what will appear to whites in South Africa to be revolutionary changes. The land must be re-distributed and allocated to those who have to live and make their living on the land. Special aid should be given to farmers in depressed areas. Each person should be allocated so much as he can cultivate himself with the help of his family. Co-operative farm settlements of a larger acreage would be encouraged and aided liberally to secure the advantages of large-scale farming.

Private enterprise, commerce and industry would be under government control as now, and probably stricter. State control should be extended to cover the nationalisation of some sectors.

Human rights would be entrenched in the State Constitution. All workers would enjoy unqualified trade union rights. There would be no discrimination on grounds of colour or race. There must be planned social and economic development to increase employment and raise standards of living all round. All discriminatory legislation and restrictions on legitimate freedom of movement will, of course, go. Immigration would not be limited to any one race.

It is reasonable to expect that there will be regional groupings formed in Africa, and maybe in some period these would form a federation of African states.

My government, mainly through education – directly and indirectly – would discourage the attitude of thinking in racial categories. Racism, and all forms of discrimination, would be outlawed. The question of reserving rights for minorities in a non-racial democracy should not arise. It will be sufficient if human rights for all are entrenched in the Constitution. The main thing is that the government and the people should be democratic to the core. It is relatively unimportant who is in the government. I am not opposed to any government because it is white. I am only opposed to one which is undemocratic.

I like to speak about 'a democratic majority' which should be a non-racial majority, and so could be multiracial or not. My idea is a non-racial government consisting of the best men, merit rather than colour counting. Parties, basically, should arise from a community of interests rather than from a similarity of colour. Appeals to racialism at elections would be an offence in law.

Within the orbit of my State, the individual would remain cardinal, for *the State exists for the individual* and not *the individual for the State*.

Education would be free and compulsory for all in the primary stage at first, and later up to matriculation. Substantial aid would be given to universities with a generous system for bursaries and loans to students. In technical and trade schools education would be free. Special efforts would be made to remove illiteracy. Night schools to provide working adults with facilities for part-time education in any standard would be encouraged and liberally subsidised. My South Africa would encourage the harnessing of science and technology to everyday-uses of man, and not for his destruction. It will seek to play a prominent part in bringing about the banning of nuclear warfare and in working for some degree of disarmament.

My South Africa would support the United Nations and its agencies fully, and would encourage foreign investment.

I am not opposed to any government because it is white
I am only opposed to one which is undemocratic

Chief Luthuli confined to his home, banned from receiving visitors, and forbidden to make statements or attend church services. The Chief loves farming and is spending much of his time together with his wife, Nokukhanya, cultivating his land.

The rule of law must be the basis of the administration of justice and be scrupulously respected. Citizens would have an unhampered right to appeal to the courts whenever their personal and corporate rights are invaded by any person or agency, be it the government itself. Special care would be taken to develop a police force that is civil and efficient in doing its work. The policeman must become a symbol of protection. The foundation of the defence would be a permanent force – a people's army.

Finally, the challenge to South Africa is to assist in finding and formulating a harmonious way of living by people in our multi-racial communities. What an opportunity South Africa has of leading the world in this regard!

It has been my privilege and arduous task to be in the leadership of the ANC to help pilot it at a most testing time. I became provincial President in 1951. In December 1952, I was nominated as candidate. Dr Moroka sought re-election. I won and I was still President-General when the ANC was banned in March 1960. Hardly a year has passed without some demonstrations.

Since my first ban in 1953, I have virtually been under some ban to this day, debarring me from attending gatherings and being confined to my magisterial area of Lower Tugela, Natal. The district, from my home, has a radius of about 15 miles. The two previous bans debarred me from public gatherings. The five-year one I am serving now debars me from any gatherings, public or otherwise.

I was arrested on 15 December 1956, on a charge of treason. I was committed for trial with all of the others in August 1957. My activities after release from the Treason Trial cost me my third ban. When this ban was a year old, we were detained from March to August 1960 under a State of Emergency.

When serving my detention in Pretoria gaol with many others, I was charged with burning my pass and inciting others. I was found guilty of burning my pass by way of demonstrating against a law. For this count I was sentenced to three years or £100, and for burning my pass I was sentenced to six months without the option of a fine, but suspended for three years, provided that during this period I am not charged with a similar offence. □

Albert Luthuli

South Africa since Sharpeville 1960 – 1988

The era of the black youth

One of the most remarkable developments in South Africa's contemporary history is the dramatic entrance of black youth – in the main school children – into the centre of the country's political arena. The events of 16 June 1976 were symbolic of something that had actually started much earlier. The two decades between 1960 and 1980 witnessed the progressive slide downwards in the average age and education of the new political participants: from the age of about 25 at university, to about 16 at secondary school.

There are many children in world history who have died terrible deaths during some particularly stressful historic moments. Such deaths usually carry significant meaning, hinting at the problems and values of any affected nation. For South Africa, the picture of Hector Peterson's limp young body being carried away in the arms of an angry young man in overalls, next to whom a wailing school girl is standing, conveyed a special, agonising significance. The faces of the young man and the school girl suggested something unforgettable: they showed an awesome play of pain and determined defiance.

The picture portrayed, on the one hand, the killing of a child by a very powerful army, and on the other hand, the determination of children to continue to resist and challenge that awesome military might. It was a terrible rite of passage. The displayed strength of the Army suggested, in a most telling irony, the irrelevance of its methods, while at the same time the weakness of the children revealed their remarkable strength. It was a play between authority, which represented the absence of alternative solutions, and the demand for repressed creativity to burst forth.

The picture and the experience it reflected were a confirmation of a special source of bitterness in the history of South Africa's black people: repression and its inevitable results.

What we also saw was a reversal of roles between the younger and the older generations in the townships. Where previously it had been the adults in the political arena who had inspired the young, it was now the young who inspired the old in the display of fresh zeal and passionate commitment.

What is it that led to this development, and what has been its effect on contemporary politics in South Africa?

The time for the radio newscast in most African homes used to be a very special moment. Absolute silence was demanded of everyone whenever the familiar chimes rang out announcing the South African Broadcasting Corporation's seven o'clock news. Whoever dared to speak at that moment would be severly reprimanded or ordered out of the room. The radio brought into the house news about the latest developments in the ever-threatening world ruled by white people. In this situation information, no matter how distorted, was crucial; and subjecting it to interpretation offered a sense of committed objectivity, an attempt to make sense of the world. It was in such an atmosphere that many black families received the news about the tragic events of Sharpeville. It is impossible that there was a black person anywhere who did not receive the news with a heavy sense of dread.

Particularly memorable about the Sharpeville news bulletins was the body count. The numbers increasing ominously with each news bulletin, each account signalling the impending failure of something that had promised hope and deliverance. It was not long after the shootings that photographs by *Drum* photographer Ian Berry began to give a visual confirmation of what had taken place. For most of the young at the time, the details of what may have led to the terrible shootings were less important than the terrible fact of the shootings. Intuition dictated that whatever protest may have led to the shootings was ultimately justified. The shootings themselves, however, were the message: this is what will always happen to black people who dare to make demands on the State.

This situation demanded conflicting responses: you were required to be hopeful, although many things associated with the State engendered despair; you were called upon to be proud, but experienced constant humiliation; you were expected to be intelligent, educated and civil, but encountered much that was unintelligent, ignorant and uncivil about the actions of the State, all of which nevertheless seemed to ensure the success of the State. Surely then, there must be something efficacious about obduracy, violence, ignorance, complete and uncritical identification with the group interest? Equally efficacious was the unstinting use of absolute power to attain one's goals. In the contest between what seemed formatively positive, on the one hand, and what was decidedly negative, the latter appeared to have a decisive upper hand. Thus, the children of the Sharpeville era grew up to be socialised into an overwhelming sense of historical failure. Parental guidance – in the immediacy of the home and beyond, in the neighbourhood, in the school, in church, in civic life, and nationally in the field of politics – suggesting a sense of legitimate and orderly life, dwindled to insignificance and seeming irrelevance. In its place was left a vacuum that ultimately suggested the absence of any sense of social direction. What remained was an open field of diminished possibilities. Black youths began to lead a life of systemised prohibition, characterised more by what they were not permitted to do as blacks, than by positive social goals to be achieved individually or collectively. When the banning of both the ANC and the PAC finally came, it confirmed what was intuitively expected from the logic of State behaviour.

Then came the dramatic reports of bomb blasts across the country, of pylons being blown up, of gruesome violence in the rural areas, of political activities fleeing into exile. And in the midst of all, stunning newspaper headlines about the impending arrival of the Ghanaian army to rescue black South Africans from the unbending will of apartheid. Who did not want to believe in the possibility of such an invasion? But the real pain was that everybody must have sensed the utterly remote possibility of such an event. And yet, it was a false hope that everybody nourished in spite of themselves. However, there were many young people at the time who absorbed all such reports of possible deliverance with an intuitive acceptance of the legitimacy of whatever needed to be done to bring relief.

The one really dramatic development was the activity of 'Poqo' in the Eastern Cape. The word 'Poqo' became firmly etched in youthful minds as suggesting some kind of 'terrible beauty', fraught with tremendous implications for our own lives. It was something strongly identified with, not because its significance was fully comprehended intellectually, but because it seemed profoundly connected with earlier stories of bus boycotts, the burnings of passes, the deaths in Sharpeville, the banning of political organisations and countless other acts of resistance or oppression, known or unknown. 'Freedom by 1963', was 'Poqo's' goal. 'Kill or be killed', 'Poqo' declared.

And then the Rivonia trials . . . What had all that political activity come to? What had been the point of it? The song that went 'Senzeni na maAfrica?' – 'What wrong have we done, fellow Africans?' asked the kind of rhetorical question that told of a deep sense of bewilderment and despair among the oppressed.

But there was some compensation. There were stories that some leaders had gone abroad to establish the liberation movement there to broaden the struggle internationally. There was something intriguing about Mandela having left the country without a passport and then travelling extensively internationally, taking with him the message of struggle. It was a most memorable lesson in geography, bringing the entire world into the minds of the young. For example, news about Mandela's visit to Algeria and his meeting with the legendary Ben Bella brought with it knowledge of the heroic Algerian resistance against the French, stories not irrelevant to our own experience.

Then it did not take the government long to regain the upper hand. The mass resettlement of people in Limehill hit the headlines. There were to be other areas affected: Bultfontein, Helderwater, Stinkwater, Dimbaza and so on. We read about 'superfluous' and 'redundant' people, about people 'endorsed out' of locations. The convoys of removal lorries, the dismal and desolate cities of tents, all served to engender the feeling of harassment, of being bludgeoned into submission.

The year 1960 is often said, with much justification, to be the turning point in the history of the black South African struggle for liberation. It is pointed out, for example, that the tactics of struggle changed fundamentally from a belief in protest action, to a strong belief in the efficacy of organised political violence. The ANC's saga of political activity up to that time had been that of a deep-seated belief in the politics of negotiation, petitioning, civil disobedience, boycott, and other forms of non-violent action. This saga, looked at against the unbending history of government recalcitrance, is almost tragically innocent in the remarkable strength of its moral attestation.

However, there was something else that Sharpeville did to South African politics in addition to the change of forms of the political struggle by the liberation movement. For the first time, foundations were laid for the universalisation of political interest. Sharpeville represented the extension of the limits of political involvement in the black community. With the elders in exile, in prison or banned, and the popular political movements effectively silenced, a political vacuum was created which was bound to be filled by a generation which had experienced the relative failure of their parents.

NUSAS emerged in the sixties to be by far the most visible and most powerful South African student organisation. A liberal organisation, overwhelmingly white, and drawing its membership mainly from the English-speaking universities, NUSAS consistently remained in the public eye through its vigorous protests and demonstrations in opposition to the government. It is particularly remembered for its strong line of controversial and stormy presidents. In the absence of a viable black student organisation, it became the home of many black university students.

The relationship between black and white members was a stressful one, albeit initially in a low-keyed manner. It was essentially a relationship of expediency. Black students needed an opportunity to be involved in consistently organised student activity. This is understandable, in view of the non-existent organised political activity in the black community. To many white students, the presence of blacks in Nusas may have been sufficient positive testimony to the organisation's non-racial broad-mindedness. Inevitably, despite good intentions and much goodwill, black students felt 'used'. They were outsiders, let in to participate. NUSAS was not their organisation. It remained a white organisation that allowed black membership. It was in this context that black students learned much about the strengths and limitations of white liberal attitudes.

There was another reason why black students were destined not to stay long in NUSAS. It is simply that the general socio-political pressures of the larger apartheid society were too pervasive to make it possible for NUSAS to carry out its non-racial mandate to the satisfaction of blacks who expected nothing less from NUSAS than a total disregard of apartheid. For example, the housing of black student members during NUSAS annual conferences always posed a problem, since apartheid decreed that blacks and whites would not live together in residences. The inability of NUSAS to live according to its creed when it was called upon to do so, even though it was understandable why it was unable to do so, intensified the feeling of the organisation's ultimate irrelevance to the deep interests of its black membership. Black students could not sympathise very long with the structural plight of NUSAS.

This feeling of universal estrangement on the part of blacks in a white-dominated society must have been particularly intense within the rather restricted compass of a student organisation. Many of the key leaders of the South African Students' Organisation in its early years had had some stint in NUSAS. Their characteristic revulsion against the liberal philosophy of their time was partly based on real experience. It was the experience of self-denial, of attempting to become what they were not, of shame, impotence and helplessness, of not having things under control.

SASO entered the political arena in South Africa in December 1968 and was to be formally inaugurated in July 1969 at the University of the North. Its dramatic entrance touched strong chords in the urban black community, particularly amongst the young. Especially appealing to the black students was SASO's uncompromising and defiant stand on many issues that were of central concern to young people at the time. In this, it is best for SASO and proponents of black consciousness to speak for themselves.

First there was the dramatic withdrawal of recognition of NUSAS.

There is a dichotomy between principle and practice in the organisation. We reject their basis of integration as being based on standards predominantly set by white society. It is more what the white man expects the black man to do than the other way round. We feel we do not have to prove ourselves to anybody . . . All in all SASO feels NUSAS is a national union on paper only; white in practice, it is essentially a white English student's organisation. (Barney Pityana)

Then SASO defined and proclaimed its own image:

SASO is a black student organisation working for the liber-

ation of the black man, first from psychological oppression by themselves through inferiority complexes and secondly from physical oppression occurring out of living in a white racist society.

We define black people as those who are by law or tradition, politically, economically and socially discriminated against as a group in South African society, and identifying themselves as a unit in the struggle towards the realisation of their aspirations. (SASO Policy Manifesto)

Nothing less than the complete transformation of South African society was called for by SASO. It was as if the option of violence – now the declared objective of both the ANC and the PAC – as the dialectical opposite of peaceful protest required, in order to be successful, a fresh conceptualisation of the national problem and the desired goals:

Blacks no longer seek to reform the system because so doing implies acceptance of the major points around which the system revolves. Blacks are out to completely transform the system and to make of it what they wish. (Steve Biko)

Those were exciting times for thousands of black university students. There was a new self-confident bearing; the sensing of such strength as would allow them to challenge the world. This development was irreversible. It was reflected in the qualities of some of the early leaders of the movement who, individually and collectively, personified the diverse nature of the spirit of the time. There was the direct, unmediated and almost unselfconscious bravura of Onkgopotse Tiro, who gave the impression of someone who was ready to lead headlong into whatever dangers lay ahead. There was Barney Pityana's sturdy and unpretentious intellect which, because of its absolutely convincing integrity, enabled him to corrode the stiffest opposition. There was also Ranwedzi Nengwekhulu, with his arrogant drive; Keith Mokoape's unstinting, uncompromising and brave demands for absolute solutions; Mamphela Ramphele's intimidating female independence, and many others. Of course, there was Steve Biko, who seemed to combine in himself all these remarkable qualities. Above all, the strength and incisiveness of his intellect and his uncompromising assertion of principle, all went together with the display of the most amazing compassion. He was a man of his times, in whom was crystallised many of the hopes and anxieties of his generation. The glory of his living testimony was to be matched by the horror of his death.

Jimmy Kruger, the then Minister of Justice, remarked to the Transvaal Congress of the National Party, two days after Steve Biko died: 'I am not glad and I am not sorry about Mr Biko. He leaves me cold.' This remark has gone down as an indelible mark on the moral history of the Afrikaner National Party. It also underscored the absence of any notion of political magnanimity in the racist government's attitude towards a black leader. The verdict at the inquest into Steve Biko's death was equally an indelible mark on judicial practice under apartheid. 'The available evidence,' declared Magistrate Prins, 'does not prove that the death was brought about by any act or omission amounting to an offence on the part of any person. That completes this inquest. The Court will adjourn now.' That very day after the judgement, Magistrate Prins gave a press interview in which he said: 'To me it was just another death. It was a job like any other'. But the unsubstantiated verdict left many questions unanswered, underlining the Court's indifference to the high level of public concern.

The death of Steve Biko and the mass bannings of nineteen black consciousness organisations led to the consolidation of something that had been signalled by the events of 16 June 1976. The older generation of students gave way to the politicisation of the high schools, of the townships, and later, the involvement of even primary school children. This development had been encouraged by SASO and other black consciousness organisations which assisted in organising high school children into the South African Students' Movement (SASM). By the time the older organisations had been banned, the seeds for the continuation of student mobilisation had been planted. The growth gathered its own momentum. This development meant the effective broadening of the base of political consciousness, making the average black child far more politically involved than the average white child.

The activities of the youth are today part of a broad democratic movement which involves the reorganisation and restructuring of adult political activity in the form of the trade union movement, and the political activities of such organisations as the United Democratic Front, the

Azanian People's Organisation, the Civic Associations and others. The participation of the young in political activities is a legitimate occurrence. This has led to a fundamental revision of social attitudes towards the nature of the relationship between adults and the young in black urban centres of South Africa. The strain between the generations is still there, but there is a greater recognition by adults that their children are fellow participants in the struggle.

By the time the ANC and the PAC were banned, the system of Bantu Education had been in operation for seven years. Many of those who were to be active participants in the events of June 1976 had not yet started school. They were destined to enroll in a school system that did not make black life the subject of serious study and systematic contemplation. They were never to know, except through personal effort or the conscious efforts of progressive cultural organisations, that black people had a history, a culture and customs to be proud of; they had writers, musicians, artists who could stand with the best in the world.

Culturally the 1960s was the era of the Jazz Festival, the cinema, the soccer league, expensive helicopter weddings. It was not, however, a good time for the written word. Most of the major black writers were in exile, their books were banned. Here we recall the names of Ezekiel Mphahlele, Bloke Modisane, Can Themba, Arthur Maimane, Alex la Guma, Dennis Brutus and Keorapetse Kgositsile. The period even witnessed a qualitative decline in black journalism. *Drum* magazine lost its spirit and vigour. Many teachers who would have kept vital memories alive had gone to Ghana, Nigeria and other African countries. All in all, the school system for the average member of the 16 June 1976 generation was a place of intellectual and cultural poverty. School sports and musical competitions were still there, but something of the old fire – in particular, in pursuit of musical excellence – had gone.

Certainly, the advent of the black consciousness era gave birth to renewed cultural expression. Many cultural groups were established in the townships. Numerous groups of writers, dramatists, artists and musicians flourished in townships throughout the country. Many of these were named in various issues of *Staffrider*, a popular magazine that broke the silence enforced on the written word. Of course, writers such as Oswald Mtshali and Wally Serote had already broken the ice. But the magnitude of cultural activity that burst forth in the mid-Seventies could not have been easily anticipated.

Basically what we have only just barely had a glimpse of was the era of South Africa's black young people. But theirs was energy largely without the mature guidance of long experience. So much has happened and continues to happen in the country which calls for much higher levels of understanding as to what is at stake. It was impossible that the young could successfully run efficient civic affairs by themselves over an extended period of time. Their apprenticeship in national political activism (school boycotts, consumer boycotts, confrontations with the Army) was an investment in public political concern that has some positive implications for democratic practice. They must be given all the education to compensate effectively for what they lack.

For example, what sense are they supposed to make of all the developments that are taking place in the country in every sphere of human activity? They witness the phenomenon of multi-racial private schools; the encouragement of black business and the growth of a black executive corporate culture; the call for the privatisation of the economy; and, most recently, the granting of property rights to blacks in the urban areas. What are they to make of all this? More than ever, the young need highly developed intellectual skills to enable them to make critical sense of the world around them, and then to work out creative and viable alternatives. What hope is there that the present educational and political environment can provide them with such skills? Frankly, there is not much.

At the end of the day, we are still left with future adults who have only one major vested interest; the end of white domination in whatever manner that could be achieved. As the future stares at us, we feel a deep longing for it, even if everything makes it difficult for us to envision it.

Professor Njabulo S Ndebele

Cape Town: 11 February 1990

Nelson Mandela is released from prison

Photograph by Paul Weinberg (Afrapix)

Nelson Mandela for the first time in 27 years faces the press and the world.

Throughout South Africa the people celebrate

Photograph by Sue Kramer (Afrapix)

Celebrating the release of Nelson Mandela in Hillbrow, Johannesburg.

Photograph by Chris Ledochowski (Afrapix)

Nelson Mandela addresses a Cape Town crowd on the evening of his release.

It was a typical Cape summer's day, scorching hot. But unlike other summer Sunday afternoons, when the Cape's open beaches are packed to capacity, this day, 11 February, was very special.

A moment in time that the whole world had been waiting for since five o'clock the previous day.

It was the day South Africa's best-known, and most admired son, Nelson Rolihlahla Mandela, was to be released after having spent twenty-seven years in jail.

And nowhere was the fervour stronger than in Cape Town, for some fifty kilometres away in Paarl, where the town's large farming population mostly seem more interested in the upkeep of the sprawling, lush lawns surrounding their large Dutch-styled homes, their precious vines and rugby than the injustices that prevail in this country, Mr Mandela was to be released from the Victor

Soweto 13 February 1990

Photograph by Cedric Nunn (Afrapix)

At the rally for Nelson Mandela, Orlando Stadium, Soweto.

Verster prison.

The prison, nestled snugly below a beautiful mountain range and surrounded by the area's wealthy farmers, had been 'home' for Mr Mandela for just over a year, after he had spent much of the other twenty-five years on Robben Island.

When Mr Mandela and ten others first appeared in the Rivonia treason trial on 9 October 1963, their appearance shared the news headlines in this country with the marriage of Port Elizabeth singer Danny Williams to a white British woman called Bobbi Carole.

But let's go back to the day most of the world had been waiting for, 11 February.

When State President F W de Klerk finally made the long-awaited announcement late the previous day that Mr Mandela would be released at three o'clock on Sunday,

Nelson and Winnie Mandela arriving at the Welcome Home rally, Soweto

Photograph by Gill de Vlieg (Afrapix)

Cape Town, noted for its 'laid back' style of life, moved into a kind of frenzy that had never been experienced before.

With hooters blaring, impromptu parties being organised all over the townships and busloads of ordinary folk riding around the Sea Point area with ANC flags and clenched fists protruding through the windows, shouting 'Viva Mandela' and 'Viva ANC!', Cape Town had suddenly come alive.

In fact, not even the peace declaration after World War II compared with the excitement that was generated by the announcement of Mr Mandela's release.

Taverners in the townships of Langa, Guguletu and Nyanga reported that they were 'dry' long before the witching midnight hour.

One taverner told *Drum:* 'You would think the world is

Nelson Mandela greets a friend at the Welcome Home rally in Soweto.

Winnie, Nelson Mandela and Walter Sisulu, the Old Guard together again

Photographs by Anna Zieminski (Afrapix)

coming to an end tomorrow at three. I'm completely sold out of everything I had in stock, and I'm not the only one. And can you blame the people, for tomorrow will be the most joyous day in the history of black South Africans because their long-lost father is returning.'

With fireworks punctuating the cool evening air and thousands of people making arrangements to travel to Paarl to witness one of the greatest events in this country's history, Cape Town simply refused to sleep that night.

Hundreds of international press photographers and journalists camped outside the prison in order to get the best possible vantage point so that they could get the 'first' pictures of the famous prisoner, pictures that would earn them thousands of American dollars.

With the sun beating down on the multitude who had congregated outside the gates to the entrance of the Victor Verster prison and the many thousands more who had lined the route from Paarl to Grand Parade in Cape Town, it was to be a long wait, but a moment nobody was prepared to miss, irrespective of the scorching heat.

Policemen, photographers, journalists and followers all shared the same tap in an effort to quench their thirst.

In fact, the long wait in the sun was all about sharing. People joked. They sang. They shouted slogans. They laughed. They cried. They fainted. But never an incident.

The police, who kept a low profile while the UDF

Photograph by Afrapix

Photograph by Steve Hilton Barber (Afrapix)

marshals controlled the wildly excited crowd, were left amazed at the discipline that prevailed.

With the magic hour of three o'clock finally having arrived, one could almost feel the electricity that was being generated from an audience, of which most were not even born when Mr Mandela was sentenced to his long prison term.

At two minutes past three, Mrs Winnie Mandela and her entourage arrived at the gates below slowly making their way down the one hundred metre drive to Mr Mandela's 'home'.

The singing became louder. The slogans became stronger. The excitement reached fever pitch. Control became more difficult. But still no Mr Mandela.

'Please be patient,' UDF marshals shouted.

'We've been patient for twenty-seven years,' shouted back a young, khaki-clad ANC member, much to the delight of those within hearing distance.

'They are an hour late,' shouted someone else and the response from a neighbour was immediate, 'I hope they have not changed their minds.'

Then it all happened.

It was just after four when Mr Mandela and his wife Winnie, holding hands and waving to a now delirious crowd, alighted from a black limousine and walked the few metres to the gates.

Pandemonium broke loose as people and the press surged forward for a glimpse of a face that the whole world had been wanting to see for twenty-seven years and one that everybody hopes will bring peace and harmony to this troubled country of ours.

At first one sensed a touch of nervousness and uncertainty about Mr Mandela's behaviour, almost as if he seemed uncertain whether to smile or cry.

But having been encouraged by Winnie to raise his right arm and show a clenched fist, it must have been the first time in all those many years that he really realised he was in actual fact a free man.

As it turned out, the crowd had only about five minutes in which to feast its eyes on the tall figure of their hero with his black and grey hair and impeccably dressed in a conservative grey suit.

But at moments like these, length of time is irrelevant, for they have been privileged to actually see the man who

"Long live Mandela" they shouted, "Viva ANC!"

Photograph by Cedric Nunn (Afrapix)

Far left: ANC supporters outside Victor Verster prison waiting to greet Nelson Mandela.

Left: Nelson Mandela at the Soweto rally.

Right: Nelson Mandela at the Bloemfontein rally on 25 February 1990.

is sure to cast a larger than life shadow on South African politics for the rest of our lives and on the lives of all those who are destined to follow us.

Then followed a slow and tedious journey to Cape Town for the Mandelas.

Thousands, both black and white, lined the route from Paarl to the Grand Parade, waving ANC flags and shouting good wishes, and one wonders whether in his wildest dreams Mr Mandela ever expected to receive such a huge and warm welcome from the people of Cape Town.

There was a poignant moment during the three-hour drive when Mr Mandela bounced a baby boy on his knee while his cavalcade was held up in a traffic jam.

The incident occurred near the University of Cape Town when a woman rushed into a friend's home to tell them that Mr Mandela was in a car outside.

A man, holding a baby, came rusing out of the house and Mr Mandela asked for the child, who was then passed through the window where Mr Mandela bounced him on his knee.

At one time the organisers estimated the crowd to be a quarter-million strong, but because of the intense heat and cramped space on Grand Parade and its surrounds, about half the crowd opted to return home to their television sets when it became known that Mr Mandela would not be arriving at the City Hall to deliver his first speech in twenty-seven years before seven o'clock.

His eventual arrival was greeted with deafening applause, a sound that rang so sweetly and sincerely that it brought tears to the eyes of thousands.

When Mr Mandela began to read his speech in the fading light, the people of Cape Town clung onto every word he said with intermittent shouts of 'Long live Mandela!' and 'Viva ANC!'

After having completed his speech in near darkness, a white bank of cloud hovered above Table Mountain before settling on the mountain like a table cloth, ready to serve a man who has sacrificed the better part of his life for the cause of justice.

Yes, the people of the Mother City had done their duty by paying homage to a man who will go down in history as South Africa's greatest son.

René du Preez

Some of the writers, photographers and editors from the pages of *Drum*

1 Peter Magubane, Jurgen Schadeberg and Bob Gosani
2 Henry 'Mr Drum' Nxumalo 
3 Anthony Sampson 
4 Dorsay Can Themba 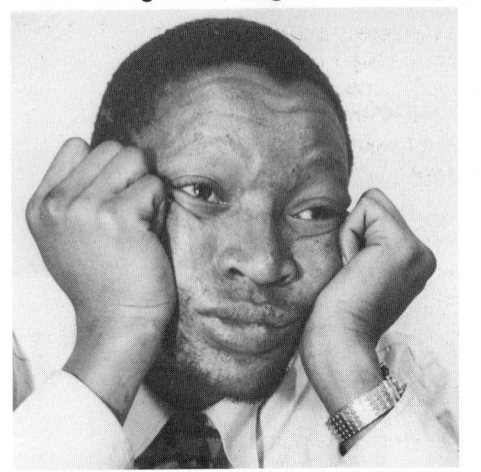
5 Sylvester Stein 
6 G R Naidoo 
7 Ezekiel Mphahlele 
8 J R A Bailey 
9 Sir Tom Hopkinson 
10 Nathaniel Nakasa 

Journalists who stood for peace, unity and nation-building

1. Peter Magubane (left) started with *Drum* in 1954 as a driver-messenger; he often drove the *Drum* team. Soon he began to carry a camera with him on these assignments, taking photographs that showed great promise and drew the attention of the editors. Within a few years Peter became top *Drum* photographer, winning many prizes and awards.

Jurgen Schadeberg was born in Berlin in 1931 and emigrated to South Africa in 1950. Jurgen joined *Drum* as the first photographer and the fourth member of the *Drum* staff in July 1951. He covered the Bethal story – the first *Drum* exposure – with Henry Nxumalo and in April he covered the Defiance Campaign. As *Drum* grew rapidly, Jurgen became more and more involved with picture editing and with teaching young blacks photography.

Bob Gosani (right) was a lanky, inarticulate 17-year-old who began his sentences with: 'The thing is'. As a telephone operator or journalist he was hopeless, but then he started to help Jurgen Schadeberg cutting up negatives and working in the darkroom. He took to photography quickly and soon produced photographs of exceptionally high standard about township life.

2. Henry 'Mr Drum' Nxumalo began to write poems, some of which were published in *The Bantu World,* when he was working for a boilermaker's shop.

During the Second World War Henry went north as a sergeant in the Army. In 1951 he joined *Drum* as the sports editor. Henry, the original 'Mr Drum', did his first investigative story by exposing farm labour conditions in the potato district of Bethal. After the Bethal exposure Henry had himself arrested under the curfew regulations, and served five days in prison writing a chilling story of prison conditions. Henry was murdered in 1957 while investigating an abortion scandal.

3. Anthony Sampson was the *Drum* editor who put *Drum* on its feet. Educated at Westminster School in London and at Oxford University, he served in the Royal Navy during the Second World War. Anthony joined *Drum* as circulation manager in 1951. At the age of twenty-five he earned £40 a month, and became editor a few months later. He possessed about the best creative brain *Drum* ever had. After a highly successful few years he moved to Fleet Street where he became one of the top names in his field.

4. Dorsay Can Themba was born on 21 June 1924 into a family of four. His parents struggled to find money to feed and educate them all. 'But I was lucky,' said Can. 'I was the first boy to be awarded the Mendi Scholarship to Fort Hare. It was a wonderful help.' After college he taught English and in his spare time read, wrote and studied for a degree in Political Philosophy. After 1952 Can was launched into journalism when he won a short story competition in *Drum*. He quit teaching and joined *Drum* as a writer. Can later became assistant editor of *Drum*. In 1962, Can von Themba, as he enjoyed calling himself, went back to teaching near Manzini in Swaziland. Then he was banned by the South African government, despite the fact that he was the most moderate of men. In September 1967, Can Themba died from coronary thrombosis while reading the newspaper in bed.

5. Sylvester Stein was *Drum* editor from 1954 to 1957, at a time when *Drum* writers and photographers were maybe at their most creative. Sylvester had a nose for good stories and it was during his editorship that 'Mr Drum' went to church, investigating apartheid in religion, and the Olympic boycott was suggested by *Drum*. Sylvester came from Durban, where he was a post office engineer, a taxi driver and a naval officer during the war.

After the war, Sylvester was an actor in London's West End. Back in South Africa he became parliamentary correspondent for the *Rand Daily Mail* and then the editor of *Drum*. Sylvester wrote a few books, one of which, *2nd Class Taxi,* was very successful. He is now the fastest man in the world over the age of sixty in the 100 metres.

6. G R Naidoo left his job as a clerk in a labour leader's office in Durban to work for *Drum* as the Natal correspondent. G R handled Durban's gangsters with superb panache. 'If you don't give me the whole story . . . the other gang will!' G R then went to East Africa to establish a *Drum* office in Nairobi. On his return to Durban, he worked for *Drum* exclusively, risking his life to get an on-the-spot story of the riots in Cato Manor. He was saved from mob-violence by someone recognising him as a man from *Drum*. He later became editor of *Drum*. G R was also an outstanding photographer.

7. Ezekiel Mphahlele 'Zeke, and ye shall find; ask and ye shall be given.' Zeke Mphahlele started off as a teacher in Natal but clashed with the Bantu Education Policy in 1952 and became *Drum's* literary editor, publishing many short stories. He was awarded his MA for a thesis on black characters in South African literature.

Together with his wife Rebecca and five children he wandered around the world as Professor of English; and after Lagos, Nairobi, Paris and Denver, he returned home to hold the Chair of African Literature at the University of the Witwatersrand.

8. J R A Bailey, a Battle of Britain fighter pilot and Africa's first publishing tycoon. 1950, fresh from Oxford, Bailey fled the foppishness of Imperial England to Cape Town, where he took control of a new magazine that would sell across the face of Africa.

'We must remember that by the late Fifties we were at the same time running four other vibrant editions of *Drum:* the Nigerian *Drum* with twenty-two offices across the most populous country in Africa; the Ghana *Drum;* the East African *Drum* and the Central African *Drum.*' At its height, *Drum* enjoyed a circulation throughout Africa of over 400 000, with around twenty readers per copy – a great mass educator.

9. Sir Tom Hopkinson edited the British magazine *Lilliput* and later *Picture Post*. After ten years on *Picture Post* he was dismissed for trying to publish Bert Hardy and James Cameron's story on the treatment of political prisoners by the South Koreans.

Tom Hopkinson joined *Drum* after the collapse of *Picture Post*. He brought with him his impeccable standards of journalism and a beautiful understanding of photography. After leaving *Drum* he ran the International Press Institute, a school for journalists across Africa, and was later knighted.

10. Nathaniel Nakasa began his career in journalism at the *Ilanga Lase Natal*. He was then invited to write for *Drum*, Johannesburg. Nat slipped easily into the artistic-intellectual set of Hillbrow. He mixed with the high, the middle, and the low. With the help of world-famous novelist, Nadine Gordimer, Nat launched *The Classic,* a literary magazine. He was the first black to write a weekly column for the Johannesburg *Rand Daily Mail*. Nat was awarded a scholarship to Harvard but was refused a passport. After serious consideration he made the decision to go, accepting exile as the price of living in the open world. After a year at Harvard he wrote extensively for several newspapers and magazines in America. Early in the morning of 14 July 1965, a bitterly depressed and homesick Nat Nakasa plunged seven floors to his death in New York.

Publications available from Bailey's African Photo Archives

Jim Bailey is issuing a number of volumes telling the story of thirty-five years of African history, recording the arrival of the African peoples and their continent on the stage of world history. From Cape Town all the way to Ethiopia on the east coast of Africa, and to Nigeria, Ghana, Sierra Leone and Liberia on the west coast. The story as told by *Drum* writers and photographers carries the immediacy and urgency of the times in which they wrote. These volumes tell of high hopes, great achievements and tragic disasters.

The Beat of *Drum*

The fascinating story of *Drum* magazine told in words and photographs by its own staff.

Foundations of the future

Original writings by some of Africa's greatest.

Profiles of Africa

A portrait gallery in words and pictures of those African personalities who shaped modern Africa.

The bedside book

A lighthearted anthology of a continent, packed full with a myriad of vignettes of African life.

The finest photos from the old *Drum*

A superb collection of photos by the *Drum* photographers conveying the humour and innocence of the time. Snippets of original text from the great *Drum* writers act as a counterpoint to the pictures.

The fifties people of South Africa

A compilation of original *Drum* articles and pictures telling the life stories of some ninety-five black personalities who shone in the fifties. It is in these people that the mood and the spirit of the angry resistance to apartheid and the wild racy Jazz Age is recaptured.

All titles available from Bailey's Photo Archives
PO Box 37, Lanseria, South Africa, 1748
Telephone (011) 659-2615